How Badly Do You Want It?

An Entrepreneur's Journey from
$5,000 to Financial Success,
And How You Can Do It Too!

GARY M. GOLDBERG

DEDICATION

To my wife, Joan, who has ridden the waves with me and has always been there when I needed her; to my children, Mark, Andrew, Justin, Victoria and Kristy; and to all of my colleagues who have made the trip so enjoyable. I simply could not have accomplished any of this without you all being there.

CONTENTS

1   My Story   Page   11

2   From the Bronx to Wall Street   Page   31

3   Traits of an Entrepreneur   Page   39

4   Building Your Business   Page   53

5   Raising Money   Page   69

6   Starting Out – The Right Attitude   Page   79

7   Hiring the Right People   Page   83

8   Motivation   Page   91

9   Taking Care of the Client   Page   111

10   Managing Your Business   Page   121

11   Being a Leader   Page   133

12   Odd Jobs, Life Lessons   Page   143

13   The Entrepreneurial Spirit   Page   149

14   An Entrepreneur's Payday   Page   159

"Dream big, work hard, treat people fairly, and this country will allow you to succeed."

Gary M. Goldberg

BECOMING AN ENTREPRENUER

I started my financial services business in 1972 with $5,000, and in 2015 sold it for a mid-eight figure sum. But I don't tell you that to impress you; I tell you that for you to be inspired. Because through all the ups and downs and roadblocks and eventual successes, I have only one regret: that I can't go back and experience every minute of it again. I want to help you achieve your goals. Not just the financial ones, but the personal ones as well, because I can tell you from experience that they're way more satisfying. Not everybody is cut out to be an entrepreneur, but if you are, you're going to have a great ride. Being an entrepreneur can be frightening, exhilarating, and potentially, totally addictive – and obviously, financially rewarding.

The earliest years, 1972.
GOLDBERG & POLEN.

CHAPTER 1

MY STORY

I n 1972 I had the idea that I'd like to open a brokerage firm in a suburban community outside of New York City, about a half-hour northwest of Manhattan. Actually, I was commuting to Wall Street as a stockbroker every day for about six months, and found that I was spending about three to four hours per day round-trip in a car and wasting a lot of time. I began to look around for a branch office for the firm that I was employed by so that I could avoid this commute. I found a location in Rockland County, New York, but the firm I was working for was reluctant to open the branch after my having found the location. They decided to concentrate their efforts in New York City. So I said to myself, "this might be a good opportunity for me to start out on my own."

At the time, I was a very young man in his twenties, with not much experience and only $5,000 available to me. That was not enough to go into business, but I called a friend of mine, David Polen, who was a stockbroker and he also had $5,000 available. I suggested we pool our money, and that's what we did. Then we went to a bank in the community and on our credit cards borrowed $5,000 dollars each to help start the business. But even that was not enough capital to start a business, so we contacted accountants and other influential individuals and told them what we intended to do. We scurried about trying to raise more money. We would meet with people in their homes and at their offices. We tried to raise $5,000 and $10,000 from people who wanted to take a shot at investing in two promising young men. We eventually raised an additional $70,000 dollars of working capital by working virtually every night on the project with investors owning about 25% of the venture. The company therefore started with $90,000.

A Kid from the Bronx

This was now quite a venture. Wow, $90,000 in the bank! Understand, my mom was a school teacher and my dad was a lawyer with a very modest practice. We had everything we needed but, like so many families in the Bronx, we never had a lot of money. One of my favorite reflections on my childhood in fact, is how my mom bought me so many clothes that were marked "Irregular" that until I got to high school, I thought "Irregular" was the name of a manufacturer.

As a kid I remember my mom taking me shopping for shoes at a store called S. Klein's on the Square. She would say, "Gary, try these on," and she'd point to the bargain bin, where there'd be hundreds of shoes, all with strings attaching the left to the right. Oftentimes, there would be something slightly wrong with them. So she would take out a pair and ask me to try them on and she'd say "Walk to me." But I couldn't walk because they were tied together with a string through the sides. I'd end up shuffling across the room and my mom would say, "How do they feel?" I'd say, "good," and that's how we'd buy shoes. I knew I'd really made it when I could buy a pair of shoes that weren't tied together with a string!

There was something special about my upbringing in The Bronx. It's what we were exposed to: either you were the children of immigrants, or your grandparents were immigrants. So there was a certain work ethic and discipline that we all grew up with.

It was just a mentality, a certain work ethic relating to success -- and to watch what you did with your money because there was no fallback. If you grew up in certain other areas, you might have had relatives to fall back on who perhaps had deeper pockets. But we didn't. I think that helped separate certain people from others.

Also, you had to work. Your nickels counted. I was brought up to make sure you shut the lights off and finished everything on your plate. I constantly heard, "people in Europe are starving. Finish everything." And you didn't make long-distance phone calls. In fact, when I arrived somewhere out of town, I would call, and ask for myself, but my parents would say I wasn't there, and then we would hang up. That way my parents knew I had arrived at my destination safely. As I said, every nickel counted.

When people came over from Europe, they settled in places like the Bronx because that's what they could afford. They couldn't move to Park Avenue, so they moved either to the Lower East Side, or to Brooklyn, or to the Bronx. And I think it helped create people like Ralph Lifshitz Lauren - a classmate of mine - and Calvin Klein and Garry Marshall (the actor and TV producer known for creating *Happy Days*, and directing films like *Pretty Woman* and *The Princess Diaries*).

When we first started the new business, it was very small. We had a fixed overhead. Our rent on the top floor of our small walk up office was $250 a month, and we hired one secretary. My partner and I took a fixed salary. Because we didn't have a reserve, we worked until the overhead was covered on a weekly basis. There was a lot to that simplicity because if we didn't cover our overhead by Friday, we came in on Saturday and Sunday and continued working until we did.

The system was perfect for us. I would go out and cold call and, being in suburbia, it was nicer than taking elevators in office buildings in the big city. So I would get in my car and drive over to a strip mall, a shopping center, or a small office building, and just start knocking on doors and introducing myself. My partner at the time – I am no longer in a partnership – would stay inside and take care of customer calls, and service the clients that we did have.

At the shopping centers I would hand out my business cards to shoppers as they left the stores. I would introduce myself and let them know that I had a new business in the community. I would approach people as they left the supermarket and walked to their cars. Then I would say:

"Hi. My name is Gary Goldberg and I've just opened a business in the community. We buy and sell stocks and bonds. Would you please use our competitive buying facilities because we're nice people to do business with!"

And that was my spiel – I can't believe I still remember it today as I repeated it so many times back then. It was not intimidating, and people would almost always take my card. Then the local newspaper picked up on it, wrote a human interest piece about me in which they compared me to a political candidate running for office.

I would work all hours, speaking almost every night, for almost any organization, and we built our business… slowly.

After a short time in our fledgling business, I thought it would be a good idea to have our secretary make appointments for me with attorneys and accountants. I would pay her a five-dollar bonus for every appointment that she could get for me. Then I decided to give her a $25 bonus for every speaking engagement that she could get for me at a Rotary, or a temple, or a church. She could use the money, so the incentive was there for her; and that's how it all began. I would go anywhere that it took to get my message out and it didn't matter, the time or the day. Give me two people on a street corner who would listen to me, and that was the equivalent of a crowd.

Hard work was nothing new for me. When I went to college, I had several jobs. Bard College had offered me a partial scholarship, so even though I was admitted to some bigger schools, I took it. The partial scholarship had the requirement that I work at the school, so I had a number of jobs. This included being a waiter. I got paid a nickel a person, four people at four tables, so I'd make 80 cents a meal - I remember it so clearly. Then I worked in the library, and I was a model in a Life Drawing class! It paid a buck and a quarter an hour. A lot more than 80 cents a meal!

I also created a bagel route at Bard. I would walk around the student buildings at 8:30 or 9 o'clock at night, with a bunch of bagels and cream cheese, and sell them to the students studying or playing poker. That was entrepreneurial right there. You had to do what you had to do.

I learned a lot by going to a small college. I've had very successful people in my firm who didn't go to a fancy school, but because of their abilities, they achieved success. In fact, nowadays a lot of people are better off not going to college, but rather, getting a vocational degree. There's a need for electricians, and plumbers and other people who have learned a trade.

It's not a matter of whether you went to an Ivy League school, but whether you have perseverance and the discipline you need in order to be an entrepreneur.

A degree doesn't determine whether you won't take "no" for an answer, or whether you'll be well organized, or not be embarrassed about having to do certain things. Those are more important attributes in achieving your goals. In sum, you don't need a college degree to be a successful entrepreneur.

Ultimately, when I became successful, I made a donation to Bard College that was a "Thank You" for all the assistance that they gave me -- and they named the computer center after me. That was a very special day in my life. I wish my parents had lived to see it.

Creativity

As an entrepreneur, it's important to be creative – and I did something rather creative. About two years into the venture and with a modicum of success, I read about an electronic Dow Jones sign that stood about 20 feet high and that could be placed outdoors and bare up under all weather conditions. I could also put my company name on it. Also, it could be leased so it wasn't too expensive. Besides, I viewed that sign as an investment, not as an expense. It gave the current status of the Dow Jones Industrials to the busy street right infront of our office, which is where I placed it. It was adjusted manually, so every 15 minutes or so I would change the sign allowing the people driving by to see how the stock market was doing. Invariably, they would drive by on purpose – remember, this was before cell phones and CNBC, as well as the internet -- just to see it and get an update on their investments.

This was also the era of CB radios. Drivers would call each other on their CB's, "Breaker 1-9, say, are you near that Gary Goldberg sign on Route 59? How's the market doing?" That really started to put us on the map. And do you know what that is called? Free advertising, the best kind.

Back in 1973, there was also a lot of fear in the market. So I had the idea that since people were afraid to invest in stocks, I would offer them the opportunity to buy Treasury Bills by simply coming to my office. For a fee, I would go personally to the Federal Reserve in Manhattan and buy the Treasury notes on their behalves and save them the trip. I would purchase $10,000 or $25,000 Treasury Notes for them – or whatever amount they wanted – and I would charge just $25 no matter what the amount was. I would bundle clients orders, and then go down to the Federal Reserve and make the purchase.

And guess what? We got an account out of virtually each one of those individuals. We would deliver the Treasury notes to them, and they were very grateful for the service. And then we would talk to them about the other services that we offered. It was an introduction and it was an attraction that nobody else was offering. We had our foot in the door, and we were in fact "nice people to do business with."

Full Service

One big turning point in the growth of the firm came in 1975. I was invited to attend the first convention of Certified Financial Planners. There were a few hundred planners gathered in Atlanta. I realized that a full service brokerage firm including financial planning was really the future of the business. I had attended law school for 1 ½ years, and had been in the real estate management business, so this combined law school/real estate/stock brokerage background all rolled into one profession – well, it was natural for me to get excited about it.

I then came back to the office and told my partner about it. Unfortunately, he was less excited, and ultimately it was the reason that I bought his interest out. He wanted to focus more on stocks and I wanted to take the financial planning approach. In 1978, I purchased his half of the business for about $125,000. As it turned out, the remaining original investors wanted to sell because they saw the two of us breaking up as possibly being detrimental to their investment. So, I bought them out as well and returned their money to them with a profit and set out on my own. (My former partner ended up managing pension fund money in the state of Florida and became successful on his own. Unfortunately, he died prematurely.) Eventually I decided that if clients could have their investment planning advice, estate planning advice, and accounting advice, all under one roof, with experts in various departments who could meet with them, then they would gravitate towards that concept. So I hired, full-time, a staff that included two CPAs, one attorney, and created an insurance department headed by a Chartered Life Underwriter (CLU).

Tax Department

One of the best things that I did was start the tax department. It made sense that if people were investing their money with me, they should be able to coordinate their investments addressing their tax requirements without one person jousting with another for control. Even today I review tax returns first, to determine what the client's tax requirements or parameters are. Frankly, I don't know how a financial advisor can make recommendations without reviewing a person's tax return. It becomes a roadmap for providing appropriate financial advice.

The Mansion

It's incredible to imagine from these rather humble beginnings that I've just described to you that I was fortunate enough to be able to purchase the original home of Thomas Fortune Ryan, a turn of the century tycoon, who in 1901 built this 30,000 square foot mansion for himself and his wife. In 1984 I purchased this 44-room edifice designed by Stanford White, the noted architect, who also designed the Vanderbilt Mansion, the Roosevelt Mansion, buildings at the University of Virginia, and many other distinctive commercial and residential buildings throughout the country. I named it The Montebello Mansion (our address is 75 Montebello Road, Montebello, NY) when I bought it. It sat on 28 acres. I eventually sold off some of the acreage to recapture my seven-figure investment. (Yes, seven figures. I leveraged myself extensively in order to make the purchase, but for a good reason. I viewed the purchase as an investment, not as an expense -- an important distinction for an entrepreneur to make.) It is truly a remarkable building, a far cry from the $250 a month walk up which was my first office. Now, when prospective clients visit, they get the feeling that we have accomplished things for our clients and that the business has been built through good performance and satisfied clients, which, I might add, is a fact. It also represents success.

The fireplaces are warm and inviting in the winter, and the gardens are beautiful in the spring and summer. It's a great place for my staff to work and it's a wonderful environment in which to meet with clients. This is our main office, although we do have branches in eight different locations. This old mansion would have gone under the wrecking ball if I had not bought it. but we both got lucky; the mansion was saved and I had an amazing new office. When I purchased it, the New York Times did a front page story about it in their Sunday real estate section, with a picture of the mansion. I also had it designated as a historical landmark.

My big concern was that some of my clients might have been intimidated by it, so I decided that I would make it non-threatening. The way to do that, I felt, was to have outdoor concerts on the lawn for the public, sort of a mini Woodstock. So every year (up until a few years ago) I would organize an outdoor Gary Goldberg Financial Services Jazz Festival called "Music at the Mansion" held on our property. We would have top notch professionals such as Grover Washington, Jr., Spyro Gyra, Kenny Rankin and on and on. It was very well publicized and all the gross proceeds went to local charitable organizations. The point was that people who would otherwise be intimidated by the building felt very comfortable coming to the property.

We found that a lot of people at the concert would ask, what does Gary Goldberg Financial Services do? So we ended up having people come to us for financial planning and investment ideas as a result. The primary purpose was to raise money for local charities and do good things for the community and get our name out there. The secondary idea was to make our office accessible and comfortable for prospects, and ultimately business came our way.

Unfortunately, the traffic that this success created became a problem in our town because we would have as many as 4,000 people clogging our local roads, and so I was asked by the town not to do it anymore. Instead, I write a check to a charity every year. I also have a golf tournament named after me, and it benefits many local charities.

The GGFS Roundtable

After purchasing the mansion, I developed another concept at Gary Goldberg Financial Services that we called the "Financial Planning Roundtable" which was held once a week. Our staff gathered around a huge, King Arthur's style roundtable, designed and built for the office. What we then did was anonymously discuss cases using first names only of potential clients, and everyone had input. We had a case study that would analyze the goals and aspirations of the client, their tax and estate consequences, and we had our financial planners – as well as the trainees who learned at this table – analyze the case. We then went back and provided a report to the client as to what the team had determined was in their best interest. And we didn't charge for the service. It became part of the value added services that we provided. We still do this, but on a less frequent basis as our advisors are spread amongst our various offices. But it still remains a beneficial exercise for many of our clients. The idea for the round table came to me because the staff was available and I thought, "Why not have everyone sit in and have a cross-fertilization of ideas?"

The majority of the prospective clients are extremely impressed and proceed with the implementation of the plan. A few might say, "thanks" and we never hear from them again, but if that's the case, we always ask them to please tell us why they chose not to do business with us. Sometimes we learn that individuals just wanted to pick our brains, but it's rare.

The Best Performing Mutual Funds

As to the development of my business, it became apparent to me a number of years ago that mutual funds were a proper vehicle within which to manage a portion of my clients' money. As a result of that realization, we have developed systems within our research department to determine which are truly the best managed mutual funds in the universe of mutual funds. Then, through a software program that was developed for us and by us, we end up tracking, for an annual fee, the best managed mutual funds and exchange traded funds that exist. And we move the money that our clients have entrusted to us into the best no load or commission-waived mutual funds and ETF's that exist.

We have a significant amount of money under that management program and we end up giving our clients the best of all worlds using mutual funds and ETF's that have performed exceptionally well.

The Buster Program

We then created our personalized stock portfolios after careful research by our in-house team of research analysts, and named them "The Buster" programs. They have been highly publicized and praised in the national press. I can easily say that the best thing that happened to me was the realization that I was not going to be the best stock picker in America. We, however, as a committee, can analyze some of the best mutual funds and individual stock opportunities. As a result, our clients have enjoyed the benefits of our investment committee choices in our 15 investment programs.

We bring in more than $100 million a year in assets. We have thousands of active clients who hear from us regularly. We successfully keep in touch with them by phone or in person on a quarterly basis as well as through a daily newsletter. My clients know we take care of their money. I started staying in touch because I understand how hard they have worked for their money and they want to know that someone is there to protect it and is keeping their eye on the ball.

Radio – for 35 years!

I also keep in touch with my clients in other unique ways. I am fortunate enough to have a radio talk show that is broadcast right from my office building where we have set up a professional broadcasting station. It is an hour-long show on several major New York stations.

(For decades it was on daily. I now do it three times per week.)

When people – especially my own clients – hear me speak for an hour on the radio, they invariably feel that they personally are "hearing" from me. It's kind of gestalt, in a way. Since I've been on the air for 35 years, some prospective clients visit the office and feel comfortable having heard me on the radio already. The program is educational, guest-oriented, and also promotes our company. And when people call and say, "You've done wonders for us and we appreciate it," it helps add credibility.

Recently, I did a creative promotion on the radio which had excellent results. I suggested to parents and grandparents that they should teach their offspring about what it meant to own a stock. For instance, I recommend stock as a great gift for birthdays, Christmas or Hanukkah. Instead of just giving a game or a doll, it's more worthwhile to gift a stock. I even composed a list of stocks that kids could relate to, whether it be McDonald's, or Amazon, which is a very expensive stock, or stocks like Microsoft, Apple, Coca Cola or Disney. I would offer to buy the shares for them and charge just a very nominal fee to cover our cost. As you would imagine, many of them, even if they had a broker, would say, "Why don't you buy it for me?" It became a good source of new clients for our advisors. Reminiscent of the early days when I was buying Treasury Notes as a loss leader.

My wife and I even do it ourselves. We bought Apple for one of our grandsons. I explained to him what it is to be a shareholder in Apple, which means in effect that when he walks into an Apple store, he is their boss! Not only can the kids learn, they feel like an owner.

Here's another example. A friend's son had a wedding in Santa Barbara, California, so my wife Joan and I gave him one share of Amazon, which at the time was $930 -- a very nice gift. The last I checked it was over $1,800. So now, not only does he feel like an of Amazon, but it can appreciate (or depreciate). Creativity never stops if you are an Entrepreneur.

Lunch with Meyer Lansky

On or off the radio, I've always appreciated a good story, and one time I had the opportunity to meet and then interview Meyer Lansky in person for about four hours. For those who don't know of his reputation, he was known as the "Mob Accountant" and the inventor of money laundering. This came about when my father mentioned to me on the phone that he wanted me to meet his "new friend" the next time I came to Florida to visit. When I asked him who it was, he told me "You'll see," and he kept it as a surprise. It turned out that my father and Meyer would walk their dogs together every evening in Miami Beach. Dad's favorite subject was "My Gary," and describing all of my perceived or real accomplishments. Meyer then said to Dad that the next time "My Gary" was coming to Florida to visit, he wanted to meet me. We ended up having a four-hour brunch together, and what an experience that was! He told me some amazing stories from his past. He was said to have interests in casinos in Las Vegas, the Bahamas and Cuba, among other places. He had been good friends with Bugsy Siegel, who was killed, the story goes, when he wasn't making enough money for the mafia, and in fact had cost overruns when building the Flamingo Hotel and Casino in Las Vegas. Legend has it that Lansky was part of the decision to get rid of Bugsy and that has been portrayed in the movie, Bugsy.

After an hour or so of chit chat, I felt comfortable enough to ask him, what he told people that he did for a living. He said he would tell them that he was a gambler. He said that he even had a business card that said, "Gambler." I said, "You had a business card?" And he said, "Yeah, we all had business cards." I said, "You mean Al Capone had a business card?" And he said, "Yeah, it said, 'Used Furniture Salesman.'"

At one point in our time together, I said, "Meyer, let me ask you a question. Are you a rich man?"

He said, "The FBI says I have a hundred million dollars."

"Do you?" I responded.

Meyer said, "No way!" So I asked him, "Do you have more or less?" And that he wouldn't answer!

I asked him the worst thing that ever happened to him, and he said he was the only Jew in the world who wasn't allowed to go to Israel. The Prime Minister of Israel, Golda Meir, wouldn't let him in under pressure from President Nixon. I asked him if it ever resolved itself, and he said yes. And he rubbed his fingers together – in other words, money. He bought his way in.

Industry Trends

Regarding our industry, it may contradict the headlines, but I feel that ethics in our business has improved considerably over what they used to be. Our industry, which is well governed by outside agencies and internal compliance as well, and the general integrity of the people who have come into this industry has witnessed a big improvement over the almost forty-plus years that I've been in the business.

There are always scam artists that make the front pages of the newspapers and headlines on TV – like Bernie Madoff -- but I believe the public has become much more educated and sophisticated. They have been able to determine who is good for them and who to stay away from, at least for the most part.

I also think the industry is generating a tremendous amount of money from the generation that is inheriting money. When I grew up there was no inheritance in my family, no pension funds, no IRA rollovers of six and seven figures. Now with the amount of money that is available to the next generation there is a self-imposed educational process that people need to take advantage of in order to help themselves manage their own money. They are forced to make decisions. They are forced to study and to read the business and financial sections of newspapers, in print and online. We are taught from kindergarten how to earn a living, but we were never taught what to do with that living as we were growing up. Now, that's becoming different, and money managers are that much more important in people's everyday lives.

So if mistakes are being made, the advice I would give to a new investor would be this: if you were going to take the time to choose a financial advisor, don't measure that person's performance on a short-term basis. Understand, when you go on a diet, you don't weigh yourself every half-hour. If you have decided that you have a five or ten-year time horizon, permit the advisor to perform for you for at least for a couple of years. If at that point you're not making the progress that you feel that you should be making, it's time to look elsewhere. I would also suggest that the client realize that the person they have engaged to manage their money is their employee. By that I mean, that every suit that I own, every vacation that I take, is paid for by our clients. So I think that a person who is starting out investing with any firm should understand that the person they are entrusting their money to should not be pompous or distant, but should be appreciative of the relationship and should be available to them. I think that very often gets lost as people become successful in my industry, and that's not fair to the investor. In my case what has kept me grounded, notwithstanding my success, is appreciating where I came from.

My background was to watch my money, like my mom and dad had done. I remember when my mom became older and moved to Miami Beach. There was a time she had a $10,000 CD that had come due, and she walked up and down Arthur Godfrey Road where all the banks were, trying to find out who offered the best gift – either CorningWare or a G.E. toaster – or maybe an eighth of a point more on a CD. My parents helped instill my values.

To be clear, they were by no means cheap, but they were aware of what the value of money was. It has allowed me to understand how important every dollar is that my clients have entrusted to me as their money manager. And it taught me to never forget:

The client is the boss.

First office location.
Rent $250 per month, with just a
bridge table and a chair.

CHAPTER 2

FROM THE BRONX TO WALL STREET

A real thrill, in 2011, was being able to walk onto the floor of the New York Stock Exchange for a six o'clock party after the market closed, commemorating our 40th anniversary as a firm, and to see a banner across the wall of the New York Stock Exchange saying, "Congratulations Gary Goldberg Financial Services," and to have all of the computers saying the same thing. It historically had a reputation as a clubby & restricted entity, and for me to look up and see that message on the wall of the New York Stock Exchange was one of the most important days of my life. It said, "You've arrived." It had nothing to do with money, but rather with a career and a recognition within my industry that I could be proud of. I also realized that it wasn't the actual business of finance that propelled me to become an entrepreneur. It was a desire to do a better job in caring for my clients.

I grew up on Davidson and Burnside Avenues in the Bronx. I can even remember my phone number! It was Burnside 7-5757. When I grew up, you didn't belong to a country club or a tennis club. We'd play in the street – stickball, punch ball, off-the-wall -- and at around 6 o'clock every night my mother would yell from the fire escape on the second floor, "Gary!" And she would throw down a brown paper bag with a sandwich or a biscuit with cream cheese on it, which was my dinner. A half-hour later she would throw down some waxed paper with a dime in it so I could buy something from the ice cream man when it was nice weather.

One year my mother was my teacher. As you can imagine, it was the worst year of my life. She came in as a substitute and never left! It was the fourth grade. And she had no sympathy for me whatsoever. In class, if nobody could answer a question, she would ask me, at age 10 or 11-years old, to stand up and answer the question. That was not a way for me to endear myself with my classmates! But that was the kind of discipline that I came from. I'm sure a lot of people, when they grew up in the Bronx, were exposed to the same discipline, which came from their immigrant parents or grandparents who were raised with it in Eastern Europe. And by the way, there were no child psychologists. Psychology at the time consisted of a whack on your backside if you didn't listen. Period.

My deepest held values came from a strong parental background. My father was a very kind, gentle man. He was a sole practitioner attorney, and he gave away most of his services. My mother, as I've mentioned, was a teacher, but she was known as "the warden" amongst my friends. She was the disciplinarian. Even when she got older she was like that with her grandkids.

One time when she was 86, and living by herself in an apartment, there was a commotion with cops and the fire department gathered outside of her building in Miami Beach. She went up to her apartment and went out on her terrace and there was a person in the unit above her, threatening to jump. She said, "What are you doing?" The young woman, in her thirties, replied, "I'm going to kill myself."

My mom said, "Why do you want to kill yourself?"

And the woman responded, "Because my boyfriend broke up with me and I have nothing to live for."

My mother then said "This is about a man? Get down from there! No man is worth it. Besides, my son is coming down in a few weeks to visit me. I'll introduce you. He does very well."

And the girl changed her mind. That story has become a family legend and was indicative of the fact that when Rose Goldberg said something, you had best listen.

Like most in my Bronx neighborhood, I wasn't very sophisticated while growing up. But in my early 20s I thought I was, but I wasn't. I remember being all excited one time because I was going to take my then girlfriend to see a Broadway show. I'd saved all my money -- I was making 50 dollars a week -- and I got great seats to a Broadway show. I couldn't wait to show off my sophistication to my girlfriend because I was taking her to a Broadway show. So here we were, sitting in the theater, front row seats if you can believe it, and the curtain went up and it turned out to be a *movie* instead of a play. Incredibly, I had front row reserved seats for a movie on Broadway! It was a level of un-sophistication beyond belief.

That same girl lived on Sutton Place in New York City, which was considered "hoity-toity." And I again saved my money to impress her on her birthday. I bought her a fancy cocktail ring that I thought was such a knockout and I went to dinner at her parents' apartment. As you can imagine I was so excited to give her this ring as a birthday present, and when she got it, she showed this wonderful excitement too -- for a moment. But then her father gave her his gift, and it was a ring with diamonds up the gazoo. It just shamed mine. I'll never forget that.

So I went home that evening and called her and I said, "It's obvious to me that we are from two different worlds, and this is not going to work." And I broke up with her that very night. The next day her mother called my mother to try to get us together again, but my mother backed me up. She agreed with me, that we were from different worlds. Sometimes it's better to just move on. It's a lesson for entrepreneurs that I learned right then and there. **If necessary, cut your losses and learn from them.**

I mean, I was a guy that once had a job grading and sorting lizard skins in the Leather District down on Gold Street in lower NYC. In fact, at one point, I asked my boss for a $5 raise per week and he turned me down. So I quit that job because he wouldn't give me that raise. What a turning point that was in my life. For all I know I might still be grading lizard skins! But I decided to set my sights higher. I was willing to take a chance even though I didn't have another job. I felt undervalued and needed to move on.

When I was growing up, my neighborhood was like a small town. You didn't leave it. If you went downtown, which was not too often, it was exciting. You took a train into Manhattan. What an adventure! Every summer, my grandparents rented a bungalow in Spring Valley, New York. You basically were surrounded by the same people you lived with in the Bronx. What a difference from the way so many "Wall Streeters" were brought up. When I finally went off the college, I realized that the whole world wasn't brought up the way that I was.

I was the youngest one in my college having graduated high school at 16. It was culture shock. First of all, students drank. In my house, while growing up, there was no drinking except for my father drinking a whiskey sour on special occasions. By the way, the extent of my mother's drinking was stealing the cherry from my father's drink. For me, it had always been cream sodas and milkshakes.

Although I was somewhat naïve and didn't know much about the "other world," I discovered that I was blessed to have some street smarts and an ability to navigate around problems when I had to face them. I also made friends easily and more importantly, I have kept many of them to this day.

Bottom line is that I basically felt that I could manage and survive in a real and competitive world.

Being different made me comfortable with who I was. That's an important quality in a leader – and an entrepreneur.

The Payoff

Eventually, my firm was bought by a private equity firm in 2015, one that wanted to get into the financial services business. They decided to buy what we had to offer, which was "Money Management for Real People" (our motto), a slogan that I created & trademarked. We serve a large base of individual clients who were not getting money management, and that is the reason for the success of my firm – giving real people an opportunity to see what professional money management is all about. I discovered a void, and decided to take advantage of the opportunity. The acquiring company recognized the unique business model that I had created and wanted to capture it. In other words, I discovered a niche – the average person was not receiving real money management. You might ask, what does that consist of? In my opinion, it is finding a professional organization that really listens to you, and addresses your needs. An organization that is not just trying to sell you a product, but instead will help their clients by understanding their needs, adjusting their portfolios, and most importantly, removing fear and emotion from a client making rash decisions when it comes to their money. I developed a business platform around that concept and got the message out. People realized the need for that approach and felt comfortable in entrusting their money to our concept of money management.

It's sort of what Ralph Lauren – another kid from the Bronx – did on a much larger scale. He discovered that regular people wanted to dress like cowboys!

CHAPTER 2

TRAITS OF AN ENTREPRENEUR

N ow that you've heard the beginning of my story, let me help you identify some the important traits of an entrepreneur.

Entrepreneurship is pursuing the full development of your potential, to see what you can become with what you've been given.

- You strive to make things better and you are willing to take action on your conclusions.
- You don't give up.
- You want to be in control of your own destiny.
- You're self-confident. (You must have confidence or other people won't believe in you.)
- You're likable or respected because of your personality and your passion. People gravitate towards you.
- An entrepreneur needs not be charismatic, but it helps; but he or she must be an effective communicator, recruiter and salesperson.
- Chances are you may not have been a good employee; and in fact, you might have been fired a number of times.

Being an entrepreneur is a lifestyle, not a job.

- It means that you are willing to work more than 60 hours a week.
- It means that getting 8 hours of sleep between 10 p.m. and 6 a.m. is obsolete.
- It means that a holiday is a working day with less interference.
- You probably sold lemonade as a kid.
- You know how quickly things can change and you're ready to make adjustments

As the legendary Malcom Forbes said: "The boss does not sleep, he rests. He is never late, he is delayed. The boss never leaves work; it's just that his presence is required elsewhere."

The first thing you need to know as an entrepreneur is what to expect, both from the road ahead and from yourself. You are going to have to build up your immunity to rejection, negativity and doubt. You must fall in love with your business. Otherwise, why would you want to put up with all the stuff? If you don't love it, you're going to fail. You'll probably give up somewhere along the way.

It is well known that Warren Buffett only invests his time and money into things that he can understand or feels competent in. He doesn't get involved in things outside his level of competence. Let that be your general guideline.

Find something you love to do, and do it well. Then figure out how to get paid for it. Identify your unique skills, talents and advantages and invest in them. Those strengths are your special gifts and identifying them is a way that you can determine if a business is right for you. Hire or engage outside people to make up for your weaknesses.

Facing Fear

Every entrepreneur starts out scared.

When I began, I was afraid that I couldn't meet my mortgage payments and other bills. That fear inspired me to hand out my card in shopping centers. It inspired me to teach at night in the adult education classes at a local community college. It inspired me to join every organization that I could in order to network. My conclusion is that **fear is a wonderful thing**. Embrace it. It brings you to new heights.

- What's fearful to you may not be fearful to someone else. So it's really how you interpret something that dictates how you will react to it.

If you see a large German Shepherd dog, are you frightened of it or do you want to pet it? Same dog, different reaction.

I was never afraid to reach out to people who contacted me in the past but never became clients, or to people who left me for one reason or another to determine why. Ask yourself, as I did, why not? What do I have to lose?

- Identify what you fear the most in generating new business. That might include rejection on the phone, public speaking, calling clients who may not be totally satisfied and DO IT over and over again until you actually look forward to doing it. It may be painful at first, but as you get used to it, you will find that you look forward to it.

Identify your Achilles heel and deal with it through repetition.

TRAITS OF AN ENTREPRENEUR

- It may be harder to reach people these days, but don't be afraid to call during dinner hours if that is part of your business model. That's when people are home. Besides, people almost always have their cell phones with them no matter where they are. Some may get upset with you, but others will make appointments and do business with you. The hours from 5-9 p.m. are "money time." If I could stand in shopping centers and introduce myself to people, as I did when I started, then these calls are a layup. Challenge yourself – make a game out of it.

- While email and computer generated calls have their place, don't be afraid of the phone – your competitors aren't using it! If you dial the phone and the other person answers, they won't eat you. If you speak in front of a group, they won't attack you. I have spoken at hundreds of seminars, in front of thousands of people. Here's a trick: Pick out one or two people in the audience and talk to them. Then expand your periphery. Fear of speaking should have no power over you. Research has shown that it is the "pre-fear" that is the most difficult thing to deal with – the anticipation of making the call or getting on stage. Just do it and it gets easier.

A public company tried to buy me in 2014. When I asked them how many brokers they employed, the answer was 13,600. When I asked where I stood in terms of my production numbers vs. the other advisors, their response was #1. I must be doing something right! That answer, by the way, partially inspired me to write this book! I felt that I had a message to deliver.

I was willing to work hard, do things that I initially did not like to do, face down my fears and forge ahead. I also practiced all of those things that I have written about in this book.

Walk out of the shadows of your own fears and you can have fun doing it. And remember failure is part of the process.

So in building your business:
  a) Pick up the phone to call the big prospect
  b) Introduce yourself at a networking meeting and
     walk up to a group of strangers and say "hi."

Believe in yourself, trust yourself and your instincts. After all, that's why you're willing to become an entrepreneur. When you take the risk, you get the return. I always realized that:

My pride was not on the line, my success in business was.

Now is a time of great opportunity. I'm here to ensure that you don't miss it. I'm here to help you rise above the doubts and seize the opportunities for yourself.

Entrepreneurs may have a moment in time when fear can pop up and when the person may think they may not be cut out for this business and that they might lose their investment or savings. Get ready for an emotional roller-coaster. But I can tell you, it's worth it.

Overcoming Roadblocks

When you're building and creating a business, how will you deal with roadblocks that are put in front of you? The answer, just deal with them.

Roadblocks will make you stronger, more capable and less fearful.

Let me tell you about one of my roadblocks. Throughout the late 1970s and 1980s, I invested part of my clients' portfolios into what was then a popular and acceptable form of investing, publicly traded oil and gas and equipment leasing, as well as real estate limited partnerships. They purported to offer a predictable cash flow, upside potential and tax benefits through depreciation on equipment or depletion allowances on oil and gas wells. However, when the tax laws changed in 1987, they were no longer a viable investment and in fact, people who invested in them, including yours truly, lost money as they became illiquid and couldn't be sold except at deep discounts from their original purchase price.

Was I afraid of what lay ahead? Of course. I had to explain what happened to my clients who obviously were unhappy with that portion of their portfolios that were in those investments. I had to rebuild my business model and product line and had to prepare for a down period in revenues and profits. But from that "wounded oyster," however, there came a pearl.

The refocus of my firm emphasizing safer and more secure investments focusing on dividend paying stocks, managed mutual funds, ETFs, managed variable annuities and marketing "money management for real people" may not have occurred to me if not for my need to change course resulting from that roadblock.

Gary Goldberg Financial Services is now managing more money than 90% of all firms in the U.S., excluding endowment funds, pension funds, and bank trust departments (bringing in over $100 million a year in new assets from ordinary people). I truly believe that this came from the need to take my firm in a different direction or fold my tent. I obviously chose the former. A far cry from $250 a month rent on the top floor of a walk up.

CHAPTER 3

- Remember, there are going to be emotional ups and downs. Analyze your own essential skills because that could make the difference between success and failure. And have a belief in yourself and your capability to pull off entrepreneurship!

That belief in yourself may be tested by those closest to you. What should you do when your friends and family try to dissuade you from becoming an entrepreneur? Most are well-meaning. They care about you and genuinely may feel that it's too dangerous for you to give up a job or gamble away money that you have accumulated and need for your retirement. My suggestion is that if you are really committed to becoming an entrepreneur, keep your resolve, and don't give up. Most likely, even in the worst case, if you dive into the entrepreneur's pool, you'll come out smarter, more resilient, more confident and perhaps with new skills. But remember the name of this book: "**How Badly Do You Want It?**" If you step forward, this adventure will change you for the better. If you're up to it, follow your dream, follow the excitement. Continue to ask yourself why you are pursuing a life of entrepreneurship. The answers will help keep you on track, and you will enjoy the ride. But you have to want it, and you have to want it badly.

Thinking like an entrepreneur

It's impossible to be creative if you are negative. Our attitudes affect our behavior. But it's also true that our behavior determines our attitudes.

One of my jobs when I was trying to "find myself" in my early twenties was selling "Bota" wineskins to high end stores like Abercrombie and

Fitch, and Saks Fifth Ave. They were high quality leather wine flasks that skiers often took with them while on the ski slopes. I recall how it was so exhilarating to get my first few orders and then reorders. Other than selling bagels to the students at Bard College, it was my first exposure to selling, and I got bitten by the success. It then became my goal to find a product that I believed in, because believing in your product by its very nature will increase your sales.

It took me a while, but financial instruments that could potentially better a person's life with dividends, interest and tax savings became my life-long work. But it all started with the Bota and the bagel! (Sounds like a Yiddish salsa group, doesn't it?)

The Lesson Is:

- Don't be dissuaded by fears, uncertainties and doubts. They are natural and must be overcome in order for you to move ahead. Acknowledge them and substitute positive thoughts.

- A strong recommendation of mine would be to make a practice of remembering your successes and good personal qualities and pay less attention to your failures. You will begin to experience more success.

- The bigger your start up team, the greater your odds of success. But stay small enough to get things done and manage your cash flow.

- People management, sales skills, product conception and delivering what is promised are all imperative requirements for success. (They can be learned, by the way.)

- Proper business thinking:
  - o Make incremental advances. Grand visions are one thing, but the cautious steps are what are needed to be taken.
  - o Stay lean and flexible. Try things out; experiment.
  - o Improve on the competition and don't create a new market prematurely. Try to start with an existing customer or customer base, and improve on recognizable products already offered to them by successful competitors.

For example, variable annuities have been around forever. We decided to manage them for our clients in order to get the best possible results. This type of management in annuities is rarely being done by our competitors. A broker typically would sell an annuity to a client and then "Set it and forget it." What an opportunity for a creative money management firm to step in and provide value added! We did so, as I saw this opportunity, and as a result, we currently have approximately $500 million dollars' worth of managed variable annuities amongst our various investment programs.

  - o Don't oppose the crowd, but think for yourself.
  - o One of the most common causes of failure is quitting when overtaken by a temporary defeat. If you are going to be successful, you MUST forge ahead.

Entrepreneurs go beyond problem solving and enter the realm of creative thinking. They are not as worried about the risks as they are enthusiastic about the opportunities.

- You must nurture relationships with clients, employees and providers of products.

- An entrepreneur thinks everything is possible – they have confidence in themselves. otherwise why would they put their money on the line?
- Entrepreneurs see opportunity when others stare blankly ahead.
- Entrepreneurs need to be decisive.
- Entrepreneurs are turned on by running their own business, controlling their own success or failure and where possible, not being constrained by a limit on wages and pointless rules.

My success has been measured by allowing people to retire with enough income so that they can live their lives in financial dignity. It has come from their hard work as well as from mine. I also have measured my success by having provided successful careers to people who have entrusted their professional lives to me by becoming my employees. I have seen them live productive and satisfying lives while they have provided opportunities to their own children in terms of their education and their children's subsequent careers.

Of course, the ultimate satisfaction comes to me when I realize through my guidance and counseling that I have enabled my clients the opportunity to provide a legacy to their own children and grandchildren. Ultimately all of this has provided me and my own family with the financial benefits that come from a professional life that proved to be extremely rewarding when I sold my organization in 2015. My stipulation to the purchaser was that "I come with the deal," as I had no intention of ever slowing down or retiring, and that all of my key people would remain, as I did not want any of them to lose their jobs – after all, I did not build the firm by myself. I felt it important to recognize that while I had no partners or children in the business, that this was not accomplished by me alone Finally, if you're fortunate enough to cash that "big check," don't allow your financial statement to be your scorecard. You will always run into people with more financial wealth than yours and you will perhaps feel unsatisfied or unaccomplished. **Don't confuse "net worth" with "self-worth" as the expression goes.**

Measure yourself by your own self-proclaimed achievements, not by the scorekeeping of someone else's goals. You know what fulfills you and what doesn't.

Let this book be an inspiration to you. Start now.

"You cannot swim for new horizons until you have the courage to lose sight of the shore."   **-- William Faulkner**

The earliest days.

CHAPTER 4

BUILDING YOUR BUSINESS

The absolute, most important thing in business is sales.

Nothing starts until you sell something!

Nine out of ten times, you may not have the best product or management or margins in the industry. But you can still be a leader in the industry. It comes down to a combination of sales, service and product all combined. Sales are so important.

Just look at McDonalds. Do they have the best hamburger in the country? No, but it's the companies that market themselves best that sell the most. Sales is king. Period.

A sale tells you if you even have a business. If you have problems in your business, sales will solve most of them. Sales will sustain and allow your company to survive. If you don't sell enough, you'll be out of business fast, and don't forget that performance and service will create new sales.

The great company has a mission, a vision, and a dream. But remember that the role of creating sales is the most important component, and the role of operations Is to support sales.

You must make full use of the tools around you. Think about it, if a rock is the only thing around, and you're in need of a hammer, use the rock to bang the nail into the wall. Don't feel inferior because others may have better tools.

When I started with $5,000, I was competing against other well-known established firms in my market. They closed, and I survived by working harder, longer hours and by innovating against their stodginess. I forced myself to make the most of what I had: time, motivation and a personality and a character that led people to like and trust me. And I serviced my clients like nobody else ever had. I have an amazing work ethic which I'm extremely proud of. I know of very few people in my industry who have read more or worked harder than I do. It's what I get paid to do!"

Be Persistent
- Call somebody you don't want to call. Or do something you don't want to do – everyday
- Go fishing when and where the fish are biting.
- Listen to what the market is telling you it needs. If you don't listen, you won't sell anything.
- If you have a good sales day, you never want to leave the office. You shouldn't want that day to end. Go for a second big sale. It's like a batter on a hitting streak in baseball.
- And don't forget the service that will maintain the loyalty of your client.

All growth depends on activity. There is no development without effort, and effort means work.

- Competition has the power to spur higher performance.
- When I started, I did not have "a book of business," no list of clients who were waiting to be served.
- I suggest that you meet people by setting up a small, invitation-only business conference for key invitees. Networking is so important. A wine tasting event with a local chef to welcome the spring or any other season are events that I have used successfully.
- And then determine if you are better off inviting the CEO, or the corporate planner of a company that you want to do business with. You might be better off with the corporate planner.
- It's one thing to create strategy, it's another to implement and execute it. When you give the responsibility to someone within your firm to get something done, you want someone with a wrench in their hands and who is willing to get their hands dirty

GGFS built its reputation on "Money Management for Real People," not just making a product sale and then walking away.

Acting like an entrepreneur

The clear majority of lost clients are not lost because of price or quality issues, but because they didn't like the human side of doing business with the prior provider of the product or service. Take advantage of others' shortfalls and don't make the same mistakes as your predecessor.

Switch the sale from a transaction to a relationship

- Go to trade conventions.
- Concentrate on meeting the top players amongst your principal competitors.
- Get involved in industry associations.
- Do community work where it can do the community and you the most good.
- Write articles for trade journals.
- Establish yourself as an industry expert. Let the local newspaper know that you are available for any timely comments. The same would hold true for radio stations.

Rejection

Don't let rejection scare you.

Here's an example that early in my life taught me some useful life lessons about rejection. When I was about 17, I was working at a summer camp in upstate New York. I was a basketball instructor there, and I was dating a girl who was a counselor at the same camp. Well at night, as people who worked there tended to do, we would go down to the lake with a flashlight and a blanket. I fancied myself as a singer and I would sing to my then girlfriend and play my guitar. Her name was Linda Goldner. One evening while on the shores of the lake, she said, "You know, you're good and my father ought to hear you sing." I said," Who's your father?" and she explained who he was. His name was George Goldner, but I had no idea how big he was in the music industry. "I'm going to arrange for you to go see him on your day off." she said. "You can go into the city and meet with him and audition for him." And I said "Great!"

So she contacted her dad and set it up. I went to his office on a Wednesday, my day off. It was in the Brill Building, the pinnacle of the music industry. Her dad turned out to be one of the most successful music producers and promoters ever. He started several music labels and they even made a musical about him called, "The Boy from New York City."

I took out my guitar and started to sing for him. After I finished, I thought I had nailed it. I was waiting for him to waive a contract in front of me begging me to sign it. But instead, he looked at me and said, "Gary, If I signed you to a contract, it would be like me serving hamburger at a steak restaurant." Pow, right in the kisser!

But then he said that he had a friend who he thought might like me. So he made a phone call while I was there and after a few pleasantries, he said, "I have a kid here who I think you're going to like," and the other guy said, "send him over."

I walked a few blocks, dragging my guitar with me, and I auditioned for his friend. And his friend liked me! Immediately, he took out a contract, but I was too young to sign it. My parents were away somewhere on a vacation, so I had to wait for them to come back. Ultimately my dad signed it, and I got a contract. I did cut a record, and had a mini career. Very mini! (Although I did appear at the "Bitter End" in New York City.)

I'm obviously writing this book as a successful financial advisor, not as a singer, but there's a lesson here.

You're going to run into people who say signing you would be like serving hamburger in a steak restaurant. But don't get dissuaded. Forge ahead.

Doing Rather Than Planning

There is a tendency to credit great planning for success. I have found that it really comes down to what you do, not what you PLAN to do that makes you successful.

There is a subtle distinction. Too much planning prevents us from acting. When we have plentiful resources, planning can do wonders. But at some point the entrepreneur has to pull the trigger. (For example, my taking on a huge debt to buy the Montebello mansion, or buying my partner out, required me to pull the trigger and take a chance.)

A desire for thoroughness may cause a greater delay in our actions. Also, if we delay our actions for too long, we have spent a lot of time planning for a world that may no longer exist. Had I planned on expanding my brokerage business which was transaction based, I would have misspent my time and money instead of focusing on the money management and the fee side of the business, which is where the industry ultimately headed. Nike's slogan, "Just do it," is a great call to action. Use it. Don't waste time in trying to put together the "perfect plan" when an adequate one will serve you well. You can adjust along the way.

Sales Approach

We don't have to beat our competitor. We have to WIN the customer!

When speaking at seminars, or when I am prospecting in general for a new client relationship, I mention my name, that of my firm, and I then say: "I'm the CEO of Gary Goldberg Financial Services, one of the finest money management firms in the country. I act as a financial advisor for my clients. I also understand that you probably work with one already." In acknowledging that there may be an existing relationship, I've headed off the prospect from saying, "I already have an advisor." You can follow up with an additional comment, depending on a particular scenario. If the market is doing badly, you can ask, "Is your advisor there when you need him? Does he or she clearly answer your questions and does he return your calls promptly?" In other words, is he proactive? If the advisor fails this test, you have your opening.

When the prospect says, "I already have an advisor" you can point out that most successful people have multiple financial advisors, just like they have multiple doctors, lawyers or banks. I will say: "For those of you who consider yourself successful, how many financial advisors do you have? Most successful people have three. It's a privilege most successful people have."

By the way, here's another approach I use: "If you are truly happy with your financial advisor, here's my card. If anything ever happens that gives you a cause for concern or if you want a second opinion, or if there's a decline in service or in performance or if your advisor leaves the industry, I would welcome hearing from you."

The details of these approaches can change depending on your business, but they're universal and can work anywhere. The key is that you're creating an opening to talk about your product or service, and that's the first step towards establishing a relationship and then making a sale. And like I said at the top of this chapter: "in business, It's all about sales and continual service!"

Friends and relatives

If you are reluctant to approach friends or relatives, you can start a conversation by saying, "I've always assumed that you do business with someone else already. I assume that they take good care of you. On the other hand, you may know some people who have not been as fortunate as you. Allow me a few minutes to explain what I do, and if you come across some of those people, you will know how I might help them." I then go into our technique of "money management for real people." I now have politely explained what I do in a third party context. I'm actually explaining how I can help someone else.

Friendship brings lots of advantages, like trust and loyalty. Ask of your friend: "When do you review the performance of the money managers that you utilize?" "Are you open to a presentation from another money manager at this time?" What you can also do is ask to see your friend's portfolio before their next meeting with their current advisor so that you can give them questions to ask of that advisor. You're now fresh in that friend's or prospect's mind when he meets with that advisor.

If your friends are business owners or managers or professionals, they will understand and appreciate what you are doing, as they themselves solicit competing bids for their own business, and your approach speaks the same language.

Keep Moving

- If you didn't reach your goals, maybe they were too aggressive.
- Make sure the plan is realistic and is working.

The essence of keeping your company growing is nonstop reinvention, because if you are in constant motion, nobody can catch you.

Reinvention is no different than changing your clothes every day. If your spouse wore the same clothes every day, after a while you'd stop looking at him or her. The concept and values of how we operate remain constant, but what the client sees should change regularly. But keep the company values. Think about it, Walmart never moved from Bentonville, Arkansas because they always wanted to remember where they came from.

More advice for starting out

- Risk is minimized when you have a team that will help you rebound. They help you keep your head when others are losing theirs.
- Make sure that you understand money. It's the life blood of your business.

If you get an appointment with a decision maker, focus on their concerns. And when it comes to fees, emphasize what you are providing. Fees to the client are important, but they need not be the most critical part of the relationship.

It's like the guy that runs into Penn Station and says, "Give me a ticket to Springfield." And the ticket agent says, "Which one? Virginia, Illinois, or Missouri?" The guy responds and says: "Give me whichever one is cheapest."

Your client doesn't want the cheapest service; he wants the best quality. If you were going in for heart surgery, or to a parachute manufacturer, or a financial advisor, don't go for the cheapest one. Results are what count!

Quality is not an accident. It takes a commitment of time, energy and resources. It's the culmination of your life's work.

Don't cut corners when it comes to building your business:

- Surf the web for industry information and current events relating to your industry.
- Get key business publications. Copy others on articles of interest in their field. Use your iPad or email.
- It's not only what you know, it's who you know. Stay in contact.

When you make a mistake, just acknowledge it and move on. Don't play the blame game.

A lesson I learned early in my career as a stockbroker was detailed in my appearance in the book, **Forbes Best Business Mistakes: How Today's Top Business Leaders Turned Missteps into Success.** It happened when I got an appointment, in my first year in the business, with Richard Ney, a Wall Street investment icon. I presented a stock idea to him which he started asking me accounting details about. I was doing great – until he asked me a question that I didn't have an answer to. I was so afraid of blowing this golden opportunity so I made something up. He looked at me and simply said, "You don't know what you're talking about. Get out." I learned from that experience that it's okay to say you don't know something and that you'll find it out. But if you bluff, you can lose a great opportunity. I've never made that mistake with my clients as a result of that experience early in my career.

- If you enjoy what you're doing, the chances are you will do it well.
- There is no such thing as a bad idea in a brainstorming session. Egos remain at the door.
- Try to recognize, as a customer, where you are not being served. From that, a business opportunity can evolve.

Branding

You must market yourself. **Remember nothing sells itself.** Create an identity or brand for yourself. For example, GGFS is "**Money Management for Real People.**" I came up with the phrase when I was speaking one Saturday morning to several hundred people at a breakfast. I was talking about how a firm like Goldman Sachs would only take those with extraordinary amounts of money, but that we give a similar service to "real people." That is quite a message, but we believe it.

Keep Moving (Continued)

- Create a time and action calendar. It helps you to stay on track.
- Evaluate your own strengths and weaknesses. Build on your strengths and hire or engage others to strengthen your weaknesses.
- You need to take chances and risks. You might end up with a scrape or two, but you can learn from those scrapes and emerge stronger.
- Inventory how you need to supplement and compensate for your own shortcomings or the things you don't like to do.
- It's okay to have people who are different from you and quite possibly smarter than you working for you. They'll certainly

be smarter in some areas. Some people can inspire, others may be better at getting things done.

- If possible, put together an advisory board of people willing to meet monthly. They must be objective and ideally experienced business people.
- Be inspired to grow. I once heard a great expression: "There is nothing in a caterpillar that tells you it's going to become a butterfly."

I read an amazing amount of trade publications: The Wall Street Journal, Barron's, Kiplinger's, the Harvard Business Review, The Economist, N.Y. Times, Forbes, just to name a few. That is evidence of my intense quest for knowledge and it's an obligation that I owe to my clients. I'm also forced to stay current for my radio show, "Money Matters." I wish that my doctor, lawyer and accountant had a radio show. I'd know they were keeping current. (*A selected guest list is on page 95.*)

Suggestions:

- I constantly jot down notes and put them in my pocket as reminders. And when I come back from a morning run, a technique that I've developed is to memorize key words that enable me to transcribe the thoughts that I had on the run into real sentences.
- As financial advisors, we don't compete on risk-taking but on risk management. That is the message that I continue to imbue in my clients.
- When you're an entrepreneur, your life can take on an imbalance. You must focus on the one task that really matters when you are building your business: striving forward.
- Never be afraid to walk away from a bad deal. There are plenty of those around.

- Business, like life, is like an ocean. There will be some good waves as well as some bad ones, but at the end of the day, you're going to ride out whatever comes your way.
- Call everybody back promptly.
- Show up for as many professional events as you can. The more you do, the more likely that new possibilities and ideas will be generated.
- You should send hand-written notes to your clients and prospects. If you become an important person, people will frame them. (A note from Jack Welch is framed in my office.) People don't frame emails or texts.

Observations

People tend not to remember as much of what you said, but they will remember how you made them feel.

There are no guarantees of success. In fact, you must expect to suffer temporary failure over and over if you are really serious about being a big success.

- When you see only problems, you're not seeing clearly.
- Problems become smaller if you don't dodge them, but instead, confront them.

If you're going to be an entrepreneur, be prepared to be pulled in many directions; by your employees, your clients, your family, your investors – you're going to be subject to spreading yourself too thin. That includes attending professional conferences and other business meetings. You might not be able to attend Little League games; you won't be able to raise your kids the way you would have with a 9-to-5 job and with weekends off. You're going to have to go to a lot of social/business engagements, and perhaps you may have a demanding spouse who feels ignored.

By the way, I have been blessed with having a wonderful wife, Joan, who is none of the above. Communication becomes critical. Ask the other person, "What would you do in these circumstances?" You can't do it all.

Recognize that some things may suffer – prioritize! And ideally, you get your spouse to be on the same page as you are.

Second office location.
Rent $500 per month.
Double my previous rent!

CHAPTER 5

RAISING MONEY

M anage every dime like it was a dollar. Nothing is scarcer than cash -- except maybe sleep -- when you are starting out.

- Raising money can be the toughest part of starting your own business.
  - a) Don't make the mistake that you need to raise an awful lot of money up front. You may have to give up too much equity before you have to.
  - b) Use your own money first – savings, home equity, you may even have to borrow up to $50,000 from your 401-k. It is somewhat risky, but don't expect others to invest in your startup if you haven't put some of your own money into the business. It shows confidence. It shows more than just "sweat equity" in the game. When I began,I found an accounting firm that believed in me and introduced me to some of their risk-taking clientele and they wrote some checks to the tune of about $70,000 in the form of preferred stock (which I ultimately repurchased from them at a profit six years after they invested).

- Should you go to your parents to raise money for your new venture?

  a) Some successful entrepreneurs have, including Jeff Bezos when he started Amazon. It's wonderful to reward those closest to you with your success. But the real question is whether or not it's fair to put your family members in the position of perhaps saying no to your new venture.

  b) Parents want their kids to succeed, and many of them will be willing to sacrifice to help make that happen. But they must be willing to invest in a venture that will be illiquid and with a high risk of a total loss.

  c) Don't ask your parents to jeopardize their retirement. They must clearly understand that they may lose their entire investment. Perhaps they can help in other ways. They can help you draw a business plan which would then allow you to get an SBA loan.

  d) The plan should include details such as identifying your target audience, uncovering what competition exists, what kind of setup and ongoing costs you are going to experience, and a projected time as to when the business will realistically become profitable.

  e) By the way, good plans require considerable research and effort, so unless the aspiring entrepreneur is willing to do the legwork and put in the effort to draw up the business plan, the parent should be reluctant to invest, as this could be an early warning sign of a lack of commitment by the new entrepreneur and therefore, an inability to run a business.

  f) You also must keep in mind family dynamics if there are siblings involved, since helping one child can foster jealousy in the others.

g) Parents don't have to make equal distributions to each child, but they may want to consider accounting for money that they have invested or given to one child in their wills or trusts.

h) Also, I would suggest that you don't keep any investment or loan to a son or daughter a secret. Engage the other siblings in the decision making. Be transparent and communicative about your decision to back your fledgling entrepreneur in order to avoid future resentment within the family.

i) Another approach for a parent, however, is to lend money to their son or daughter, rather than be an investor. The parent can establish a loan at a low interest rate, one that would meet IRS guidelines to avoid gift tax implications. In so doing, the parents would avoid potential lawsuits and other problems that may be created by the business. Remember, too, that the loan could be forgiven over time by the parents.

j) Gifting of the money is another option and most people won't have to worry about gift tax implications. People now have the ability to give away over $11 million during their lifetimes before taxes would be owed. You would have to file a gift tax return if you are gifting more than $15,000 per recipient per year or $30,000 per couple.

If you can find an accounting firm, or a law firm or a client or supplier that will benefit from your success, that becomes an excellent place to start raising money outside of friends and family and conventional financing.

Here are several recommendations to the embryonic entrepreneur:

- If you're starting a new company, if possible, secure two times the capital that you think you may need because it gives you the confidence and the strength to do what you think is right.
- Hold your fixed costs to a minimum.
- If you can, share office services and equipment.
- Use the computers and servers that you currently have.
- Consider short term leases instead of purchasing. (Short term because things become obsolete before you know it. Eventually you may be better off owning.)
- Use teleconferencing instead of travel if feasible. But don't forget, nothing beats face to face.

An example: I had a client who relocated to Florida and attended a seminar there that was put on by a financial firm. A good salesman playing the relocation card convinced my client to transfer his sizable family accounts to the local firm after he had been my client for many years. They played upon his geographical change from New York to Florida as a reason for him to change advisors. I immediately called my client and told him that I had researched what the plane schedule was to West Palm from Newark for that Saturday and that I would see him for lunch on his home turf as he was important enough for me to have a face to face meeting with him before he and his family finalized the transfer. I'm happy to say that the client never left. That could not have been done in a teleconference.

If a client is unhappy with you or leaving you, call them and confront it. Meet with them and let them know how important they are. (Press the flesh.)

There comes a point in business deals when you need to meet in person.

Additional advice:

- Hire interns from local schools who can use the money as well as the experience and the resume item.

But don't ever forget: differentiate between an expense and an investment! Don't be afraid to invest – good employees are an investment.

- Don't be afraid to negotiate. I have a favorite phrase: "The baby that doesn't cry doesn't get fed."
- Look for non-dilutive capital such as grants or loans at very low interest rates. This way you can keep the company from giving out equity unnecessarily or prematurely.
- The cost of starting a business today is a fraction of what it once was. Start-ups can do so with minimum payroll – accounting and IT can be outsourced on a project by project basis.
- Access to capital is also improving. There are "crowdfunding" websites such as "Kickstarter."
- With on-line services such as Kickstarter, understand that they can be both positive and negative. The good thing is that it's very easy to find and get interested investors if your message rings true. The bad thing is that it's easy for everybody else, too, so there's a lot of competition.
- "Shadow banking" represents direct lending by hedge funds, insurance companies and crowdfunding entities.
- Establish a line of credit, even if you don't use it. It can keep you going during cash flow crunches while you await the payment of your receivables.

- **As I have said, if you are going to go the route of family and friends, keep in mind the strains that it may create. The fact is that more than 50% of small businesses fail in their first five years. Therefore, make sure that people are investing money that they can afford to lose.**

And be sure to put any lending or equity agreement in writing with the terms clearly laid out. On the positive side, if you are successful, what better feeling is there than enriching friends and family members that believed in you?

- By the way, try to avoid using credit cards to fund your business. The 10% - 20% interest rates (at least) should be used only as a last resort. If you do go that route, you must be ultra-careful in your expenditures.
- Interview several lending institutions. Some banks will view you as a land mine. Others as a potential gold mine. Find one that has a tradition of helping start-ups and is not stodgy.
- If you use conventional financing through a bank loan, you can consider having your loan guaranteed by the Small Business Administration. They will guarantee up to 80% of the loan if you meet their criteria.
- If you are going to have a partner, make sure that you have a carefully worded buyout agreement, drafted by a lawyer, in case things don't work out the way you had hoped.
- The basics still apply. What you need to say to a potential investor is as simple as, "This is what my company does -- or will do. And this is what I intend doing to make it very successful."
- Once you are in your business, don't be afraid to spend, but do it wisely, and of course don't waste money on things that won't improve the business.

- If possible, own your own real estate. It feels better, and you have a chance for appreciation and lots of equity in the property.
- Cash is king. "With money, you can make money."
- Find outside services to use for a fraction of your internal cost.
- Find someone to do it "on the cheap," who initially will take on some of the risk for a future reward.

An added bonus is that from suppliers and customers you can find out a perspective on what needs to be changed in your industry and where opportunities may be. You should also pick the brains of people who call upon you (such as, in our industry, wholesalers for financial products like mutual funds and insurance products). What's going on in other companies and the industry? You can often find out from conversations with them where opportunities may lie.

Apartments, Houses, Offices,
Industrial Properties. Acreage,
Merchandise Offerings,
Rooms and Board
Wanted to Purchase

Copyright © 1984 The New York Times

Stanford White Mansion

Still Another Life

In recent years, many companies have found that the spacious homes and gracious estates that dot the suburban landscape suit their needs for a distinctive headquarters or a comfortable branch office much better than conventional office buildings.

Now one of the earliest of these conversions is going to be recycled again. It is Montebello, the turn-of-the-century mansion in Suffern, N.Y., that was designed by Stanford White for Thomas Fortune Ryan, the industrialist. After serving for more than 30 years as an office and records center for the Phelps Dodge Corporation, the 44-room mansion and its grounds of 28 acres were acquired recently by Gary Goldberg & Company, a financial planning concern in Spring Valley.

Gary Goldberg, the head of the company, plans to renovate the structure, which has about 34,000 square feet of usable office space, move his company into about 7,000 square feet and lease what remains.

Mr. Goldberg paid $1.6 million for the estate, which is at Hemion and Montebello Roads, and expects to spend at least $600,000 more to renovate the four-story brick house. The plans call for enclosing the front porch with glass, installing an elevator and ripping up the existing linoleum so that the hardwood floors can be refinished.

Occupancy is planned for July and space will be leased for between $20 and $22 a square foot.

The New York Times/Larry C. Morris

Montebello, a mansion in Suffern, N.Y., designed by Stanford White, is becoming a financial planning center.

CHAPTER 6

STARTING OUT - THE RIGHT ATTITUDE

C ompete like your life depends on it, because in some ways it does.

- I have found that hard work plus success equals confidence.
- The man with confidence in himself gains the confidence of others.
- You have to learn to win without bragging and learn to lose without excuses.
- Confidence is a good thing, but arrogance will do you in.
- Don't ever think you have it all figured out.
- Don't sell yourself short: it's not bragging if you can do it. Let people know of your capabilities. They will then follow you.

For a lot of people there's a reluctance to confront the issue, but you may have to deal with it. If you have a problem and you address it with the other person, you've now shifted some of the responsibility to the other person. Otherwise, it stays with you.

Don't allow a lack of formal education make you self-conscious. Some of the best ideas and most important discoveries have come from people with very little formal education (e.g., Thomas Edison).

- It's not enough to want to win, you must prepare to win. Read up on your industry trends, go to meetings and conferences and introduce yourself, and do your homework so when the time comes, you've put yourself in the right position to succeed.
- Leaders are not born, they are made, and they're made by effort and hard work.
- Even a two car parade gets fouled up if you don't decide who's going to organize.
- Give your best when you least feel like giving your best. Bosses don't call in sick!
- If things aren't working out, don't be afraid to go back to the drawing board. That's why we have drawing boards.
- If you bust, you at least will have accumulated some valuable wisdom, which you can apply to your next business venture.
- **Always remember, the key to failure is trying to please everybody.**

If you're going to work, work as hard as you can.

A wonderful motivational philosophy that I heard years ago:

Tomorrow we will reach higher, run faster and stand taller. We can and will do better.

A Growing Company (1990).

CHAPTER 7

HIRING THE RIGHT PEOPLE

O nly hire great people. Great employees make your life easier and your business better in every way. They can set you free from the administrative paperwork that you hate to do and that you're not good at.

When we hire a new employee, I call them into my office. I congratulate them, and say, guess what?

"You made the cut!"

Now let me tell you what that means. It means that if you make a mistake, you're not going to get fired, where other firms may fire you on the spot. We've made a decision that you're going to be an important component of this firm. Now, if you continue to make mistakes, we made a mistake in hiring you. But don't be afraid to take some creative chances and seek new opportunities. Show them to me or your boss before you implement, but you won't get fired if they don't work.

- If someone messes up one time, it could be bad luck; a second time, a potential bad habit; a third time, a bad choice in having hired them. It's time to make a change.
- When you hire, hire evidence of success, not first-time enthusiasm. You probably don't have the time or resources to train or develop anyone's skill or attitude.
- When you hire, look for someone who has shown success in prior work environments. Perhaps they also had leadership skills in whatever roles they had which you can then call upon.
- Get references from people they have worked for, worked with, and people they have managed. You learn a lot when you drill down.
- I've mentioned this before, but look at payroll not as an expense, but as an investment. Invest in the best quality you can get. But you must get a good return on it, otherwise it's an expense.
- If you hire the wrong person and if you add up the cost of recruiting, paying, training, maintaining and severing a poorly performing employee, along with their mistakes, missed opportunities and failures, a bad hire can be as much as ten times their annual salary.
- **Steve Jobs said: "A-players hire A-players and B-players hire C-players. We only want A-players here."**
- Like Darren Hardy said, "A-players are like a vaccine for the mediocrity virus."

You cannot afford not to hire A-players. Get the money from somewhere! You should hire smarter, more talented and more skilled people than you are. Pick the right people and keep them.

If you choose the A-players, they're free! That's because they will bring in a lot more value than they cost you.

Good employees are an investment, not an expense. (Sound familiar yet?) You first need to be sure that you provide the A-players the proper support and the right opportunities to allow them the ability to give you the right return on the investment you made in them. Talented people are expensive, but worth the investment.

- In the financial services industry, there are many firms that sell stocks, bonds, mutual funds and annuities. But what creates the distinction amongst the organizations that stand out are the people that make up the company. It is our people who make us exceptional.

It's okay to be the dumbest one in the room. The leader's first job is to get the smartest people in the room to deliver.

In choosing who to hire, do you always go with the Harvard grad over the community college grad? No! The Harvard grad may come with a silver spoon attitude rather than the appreciation of the opportunity. A lot of them have been pampered all of their lives. In a competitive situation -- and maybe this perspective is because I'm from the Bronx -- I've seen the street savvy person win more often than the silver-spooner!

I also don't look for someone with a 4.0 grade point average. Eric Brooks, the author of "Barking Up the Wrong Tree," found that the average millionaire had a college GPA of 2.9. He found that valedictorians did well in life, but they didn't become billionaires or the people who run the world in general. Instead, they followed the rules and seldom had the creativity to break out of the pack. They became part of "the system." The key characteristic of the most successful people who became business and world leaders, is that they had grit and determination. They were willing to work to succeed.

HIRING THE RIGHT PEOPLE

That's who I want on my team.

- Network your existing staff to find new employees. You're more likely to find people with similar values.
- You don't train your people to be smart or friendly; you first hire smart and friendly people. Also, you can't train people to be hard working, disciplined or loyal. It must be inherent.

Recruit character as much as you recruit ability.

- In terms of compensating great people, it's not all about the money. It's about opportunity, growth and challenge. Talk about the opportunity to work with other talented, passionate and highly motivated people. But be willing to pay for the best.
- If you're hiring Millennials, those born in the 1980s and 1990s, understand they value self-expression, not compliance; independence more than routine. And remember they're very tuned into what their friends are earning.

Don't get caught up by individuals who hold themselves up as "experts," and who will charge you a lot of money because they have degrees on their wall or have lot of books in their offices. I went through a number of outside professionals before I found the right ones. Oftentimes, it is the younger accountant or lawyer who is first starting their practice who can devote the time to you that you need and who wants to impress you with their availability that will prove to be the perfect fit. And they are probably less expensive.

Experts also come with a significant liability. They may be too rigid and may be blinded to using resources that depart from convention.

I have had my accountant and lawyer for more than 30 years. We all started together when we were young. But at the same time, I find myself dealing with members of their firms who may bring new and fresh ideas to complement the relationship.

When you hear someone say to you as the head of your company,
"It must be nice to be in charge," it isn't always nice. It's hard work.
The hours are demanding and it's emotionally hard.
You have to make the tough decisions.

When it comes to your colleagues:

- Get to know each other—what motivates each person.
- My associates don't look alike, think alike or have the same personalities, and I don't want them only thinking the way I do. Don't strive for sameness, strive for balance.

If you hire a "rock star" employee, other rock star employees will
want to join the team.

- Don't just hire people who agree with you. Include people who challenge you and are smart and will stretch you.
- Never try to teach a pig to sing. It wastes your time and annoys the pig. (I forget where I heard that, but it's true!)
- Spend more time hiring A players and less time trying to improve C players.

If you're putting together a terrific orchestra, you don't want the person who can only play the piano at the Holiday Inn.

Investment & Financial Planning Services

GARY GOLDBERG & COMPANY, INC.

75 Montebello Road
Suffern, New York 10901
914-368-2900
1-800-433-0323

Dear Investor:

I am proud to present you with Heard on the Street, a sampling of the many financial publications which have come to Gary Goldberg & Company for our advice and opinion.

These excerpts will also give you an idea of the many opportunities and questions involved with complete financial planning. Should you have any questions, please contact one of our financial planners who will be happy to help you.

Sincerely,

Gary M. Goldberg, CFP

FRIDAY, JULY 22, 1988

Advice from 3 who have made it
Rich investors urge caution in market

Baffled about how to play the stock market?

Me too. So I asked three rich fellas—all savvy, successful investors—where they're putting their bucks right now.

The trio:

• Walter Mintz, 59, co-builder of Cumberland Partners, one of New York's success stories in money management (assets: well over $500 million). The son of a Viennese lawyer, Mintz, a private investor, is worth well over $10 million.

• Fred Adler, 63, one of the USA's top venture capitalists, especially in high tech. (He helped catapult Data General and Daisy Systems). He's also a partner of Adler & Shaykin, a New York leveraged buyout firm whose slew of takeovers includes

Chicago Sun Times Inc. and Joy Mfg. Co. Adler, whose dad lost a thriving bakery business in the Depression, is said to be worth close to $100 million.

• **Gary Goldberg, 48, head of Gary Goldberg & Co. a financial planning firm in Suffern, N.Y. Bronx-born Goldberg, from a family of modest means, is worth about $22 million. His 1987 income—it should have only happened to me—ran close to $5 million.**

At this juncture, all three are wary.

Goldberg's market view: Go easy! His chief fears:

• A Dukakis victory leading to more social spending and inflation.

• Higher bond yields are now a bit over 9%. If they go to 10% — which Goldberg

says is quite possible given widespread inflationary worries — he sees a mass exodus from equities. "Who needs stocks with a 10% treasury yield?"

• A collapse of the rich Japanese market — which could also bomb other markets.

Still, Goldberg has put big bucks into four stocks.

Phillips Petroleum, American Cyanamid and Pillsbury Co. — are rated takeover, they're all worth owning on their own merits, he says. The fourth: Belmac Corp., which is selling a cure for hemorrhoids overseas and is aiming for USA marketing approval.

So the wrapup from our three rich wise men: The market may be shaky, so stick with solid stocks.

A Bronx Boy's Dream.

CHAPTER 8

MOTIVATION

Write down your definition of success. Your definition, on your own terms. What makes you really happy? What does success really look like? For me, is it the office mansion that I drive up to every day? Is it the car in my garage? Or is it the lifestyle I've provided to my clients through my advice, or the careers that I have provided to my employees, who have decided to hitch their careers to my wagon? It is definitely the latter.

- Steve Jobs said, "Your time is limited, so don't waste it living someone else's life."
- Very few people have the guts to leave the security of corporate life, the weekly corporate paycheck and their benefits.
- Entrepreneurs are often "round pegs in square holes." They see things differently and they're not satisfied with the status quo.
- Don't let others scorn your efforts or your enthusiasm. Don't let them drag you back into the herd.
- Don't just sit down and wait for appointments to come. Get up and make them happen.

- If you need to speak to someone, give them a call, even if you've already left a message.
- What makes me keep on going is not money, or fame from my radio presence or from the exposure in the press; it is that I love what I do. I love my work and I continue to help people.

When you start taking yourself too seriously, remember, when you die, the number of people who will show up for your funeral will depend on the weather. So don't live for other people's approval, and don't take yourself too seriously.

- If you can eliminate nervousness, worry and fear when calling on someone, you'll make better decisions more easily.
- There is the 18-to-65 rule. At 18, we are worried about what other people think of us; at 40, you stop worrying as much about what people think about you; at 65, you realize that people weren't thinking of you after all. They're really too busy thinking about themselves. So first, go for it. Don't be dissuaded by your fear of what others may think.
- Don't wait for things to be perfect. General Patton said: "A good solution applied with vigor now is better than a perfect solution applied ten minutes later."
- When you get knocked down, and it will happen, it's OK. Just try to reduce the time that you stay down on the mat and how frequently you land on your butt.
- If you're not falling down, chances are you're not pushing yourself hard enough. Falling down is part of getting better.

Falling down in the process of growing your business is proof that you are stretching and growing past your previous limits. Therefore, setbacks, obstacles, and rejections are nothing more than improvement markers on the journey towards success.

Appreciate them, celebrate them.

- A great haberdasher once told me, "Clothes are your wrapping. Everyone treats a beautifully wrapped gift with more reverence and care than one wrapped in a paper bag." The message is, "Don't wear scuffed shoes or wrinkled shirts. Dress for success." If you dress like a professional, you'll be respected as one.
- Locate centers of influence, people with their own large network of people.
- Instead of cold calling for business, find a relationship bridge between you and your desired client. A game of golf, an invitation to a sporting event or dinner together at a good restaurant can grow an acquaintanceship into a friendship and ultimately a business benefit.
- Substitute the word "help" in place of the word "sell" and people will be more receptive to your ideas.
- Don't hide behind "to do" lists, email checking, mindless meetings or unnecessary paperwork. Stop hiding, start selling and servicing.

The Titan of Talk Radio

Famous guests? He's got 'em, along with a unique mix of business and financial programming. Find out why Suffern's Gary Goldberg has been reeling in local listeners for 22 years

By Peter Gerstenzang

I t is just off Montebello Road in the heart of Suffern, but the mansion rises up like something that would fit comfortably among the grand old homes of Newport, Rhode Island. There are impeccably manicured grounds; pots of flowers perfectly positioned on the hillside; a parking lot that accommodates a dozen cars; even two stone lions, half-turned and silently roaring, on either side of the steps that lead visitors inside. It is easy to imagine a tuxedo-clad servant greeting you at the door. Once inside, however, your film noir fantasies fade as you realize that you've arrived at the offices of Gary Goldberg Financial Services. A longtime money manager, Goldberg is also the host of the popular, locally syndicated radio show *Money Matters* — which is broadcast live right from this stately building. In its 22nd year, the show is one of the longest-running financial programs in the nation. But after spending time with Goldberg, the mansion makes sense: This man is as unique as the century-old building where he conducts his business.

Photographs by **Gene Gouss**

Longest running financial radio talk show in America: Money Matters.

MONEY MATTER$
FINANCIAL NETWORK

Past Money Matters Guests:

John Sculley - *Former CEO, Apple*
Steve Case - *Co-Founder, AOL*
Jack Stahl - *Former CEO, Revlon; Former Pres., Coca-Cola*
Norman Lear - *TV Producer*
Richard Kovacevich - *Former CEO, Wells Fargo*
Suzanne Somers - *Actress and Entrepreneur*
Mike "Coach K" Krysheski - *Duke Basketball Coach*
Charles Bronfman - *Former Co-Chairman, Seagram;*
Dennis Hastert - *Former Speaker, U.S. House of Rep.*
Lance Armstrong - *Professional Cyclist, Cancer Survivor*
Newt Gingrich - *Former U.S. House Speaker*
Jack Lew - *U.S. Secretary of the Treasury*
Anson Williams - *Actor and Entrepreneur*
Joe Garagiola - *Former Baseball Player, TV Personality*
Jesse Ventura - *Former Governor, Minnesota*
Fran Tarkenton - *Former NFL Quarterback, Entrepreneur*
Charlie Daniels - *Country Music Star*
Mark Cuban - *Owner, Dallas Mavericks*
Todd Stottlemyre - *Former MLB Pitcher, Entrepreneur*
Peter G. Peterson - *Former U.S. Secretary of Commerce*
Elaine Chao - *U.S. Transportation Secretary; Former U.S. Labor Secretary*
Steve Forbes - *CEO, Forbes; Former Presidential Candidate*
Patrick J. Buchanan - *Former Presidential Candidate*
Rep. Charles Rangel - *Congressman; Chairman, House Ways & Means Committee*
William Bennett - *Former Secretary of Education*
Ed Koch - *Former New York City Mayor*
Sam Stovall - *Chief S&P Investment Strategist*
William Cohen - *Former U.S. Secretary of State*
Bill O'Neill - *Founder, Investor's Business Daily*
Howard Lutnik - *CEO, Cantor Fitzgerald*
Tim Zagat - *Pres. Zagat Research/Restaurant Guides*
John Stossel - *ABC News, 20/20; Fox*
Gene Pressman - *Former CEO, Barneys*
Dr. Arthur Agaston - *Founder, South Beach Diet*

John Jacob - *CEO, NASDAQ Global Services*
Ron Jaworski - *Former NFL Quarterback*
Jackie Mason - *Comedian*
Rod Carew - *Hall of Fame Baseball Player*
Fay Vincent - *Former Commissioner of MLB*
Gary Bettman - *Commissioner of NHL*
Mike Lindell - *Founder and CEO, MyPillow*
John Bogle - *Founder, The Vanguard Group*
Robert Rubin - *Former U.S. Treasury Secretary*
Jack Welch - *Former CEO, General Electric*
Phil Esposito - *NHL Hall of Famer*
Marv Levy - *NFL Hall of Fame Coach*
Andrea Mitchell - *Correspondent, ABC*
Richard "Digger" Phelps - *Basketball Coach*
Richard Belzer - *Actor*
Wayne Rogers - *Actor, Investment Guru*
Sir Richard Branson - *Founder & CEO, Virgin Atlantic*
Tom Daschle - *Former U.S. Senator*
John Hickenlooper - *Governor of Colorado*
Lincoln Chafee - *Former U.S. Senator*
Carl Bernstein - *Pulitzer Prize-winning Journalist*
Jonathan Tisch - *CEO, Loews Hotels*
Tom Delay - *Former U.S. House Majority Leader*
Robert Reich - *Former U.S. Labor Secretary*
John Whitehead - *Former Chairman, Goldman Sachs*
Jenny Craig - *World Famous Weight Loss Guru*
Muriel Siebert - *"The First Lady of Finance"*
Maria Bartiromo - *CNBC Anchor/Reporter*
David Novak - *Former CEO, YUM! Brands*
Norman Maneta - *Former U.S. Transportation Secretary*
Steven Bollenback - *Pres. & CEO, Hilton Hotels*
Jack Welch - *Former CEO, General Electric*
Stephon Marbury - *NBA; Starbury Athletic Wear*
Hugh Panero - *Former Pres. & CEO, XM Satellite Radio*
Ron Insana - *CNBC Anchorman*
Rob Orrefice - *Former CEO, Dow Chemical*
Bruce Hertzke - *Former President, Winnebago*
T. Boone Pickens - *Founder and President, BP Capitol*
Admiral James Stavridis - *Former Head of NATO*

Just some of our guests on the radio show. Is there a better way to make sure your money manager is up to date than talking to news makers?

General Norman Schwarzkopf, Jr.

Float like a butterfly, sting like a bee, the legendary Muhammed Ali.

Joe Piscopo, Entertainer, Saturday Night Live Comedian Radio Show Host.

With Israeli Prime Minister, Benjamin Netanyahu and our respective wives.

Marshall Loeb, Managing Editor of Fortune and Money Magazines, paying attention.

Hosting the longest running financial radio program, Money Matters.

GARY M. GOLDBERG

1997 RECIPIENT OF THE MERCY COLLEGE TRUSTEES' MEDAL

Mercy College Trustees' Medal

GARY M. GOLDBERG is president of Gary Goldberg & Company, Inc., a financial planning and investment services firm which he founded in 1972. He is widely recognized as a leading authority on tax advantaged investments and financial planning and his quotes have appeared in The Wall Street Journal, Forbes, Fortune, Money, Newsweek, New York Magazine, U.S.A. Today and in over 200 newspapers throughout the country. He hosts his own daily financial radio talk show "Money Matters," on WFAS AM and co-authored the book, High Powered Investing: A financial planner's guide to making money in today's uncertain markets.

Beginning his career offering brokerage services only, he soon recognized his clients' need for professional assistance and help in determining appropriate financial objectives and implementation to fulfill those goals. Long before the term "financial planner" came into vogue. Gary was advising and guiding his clients in important financial planning. The firm currently advises thousands of corporate and individual clients in 35 states and 12 countries.

Mr. Goldberg was elected to the Mercy College Board of Trustees in 1993, the same year his son graduated Mercy College. He has been a generous friend and supporter of the College, and in 1997 was a major sponsor for the inaugural Mercy College Annual Golf Outing. He has also been an active participant in community affairs in and around Westchester County.

Mercy College is pleased to bestow its prestigious Trustees' Medal on Gary Goldberg and to honor his commitment and dedication to our students.

Program description of the Mercy College Award Dinner.

**Music at the Mansion.
Our very own Woodstock!**

APRIL 22, 1991
VOLUME 74, NO. 15

50

BREAK OUT THE BUBBLY

After majoring in football at Toledo, tight end Jerry Evans will
almost certainly be celebrating on NFL draft day
BY DOUGLAS S. LOONEY

INDIANAPOLIS

It's put-up-or-shut-up time. This is the National Football League Scouting Combine, where potential pros are pushed, poked, X-rayed, questioned, explored, criticized, measured, weighed, timed, evaluated, stretched, rubbed, ogled. And a bunch of other stuff. "This," Evans says, "is the ultimate meat market." It is completely dehumanizing. Hyperbole doesn't cut it here. Performance does. Evans stays at the Holiday Inn for his three-day session, Feb. 8-10. They are three momentous days. These are the days of his life.

He proceeds to shoot out the lights. His numbers are magnificent. He bench-presses 225 pounds a whopping 30 times, best among the 22 tight ends. The average for the tight ends is 19. (Mark Bavaro of Notre Dame and the Giants, who was a serious weightlifter, did 27 in 1985.) Evans receives a score of 89% in receiving drills, not only the best among all the tight ends but best among the 82 receivers in all positions. About 50 balls are thrown to him. He doesn't drop one. Times on the spongy surface are slow. Average for the tight ends is 4.95 seconds; Evans is 4.8, fourth-fastest.

Evans, Tight-End from Toledo University felt honored that a wealthy
man like Gary M. Goldberg wanted to help plan his financial future.

SUFFERN, N.Y.

On Dec. 27, Evans flies to New York with his parents to meet a financial planner, Gary M. Goldberg. "He's a very busy man," says Jerry junior, "a very wealthy man. It was an honor for this guy to want to talk to me. I thought he was warm, honest, a great human being." Yeah, muses young Evans, maybe Goldberg is the one.

My daughter, Actress, Victoria Profeta.

My daughter, Dr. Kristine Gedroic MD

40th Anniversary of Gary Goldberg Financial Services on the floor of the New York Stock Exchange.

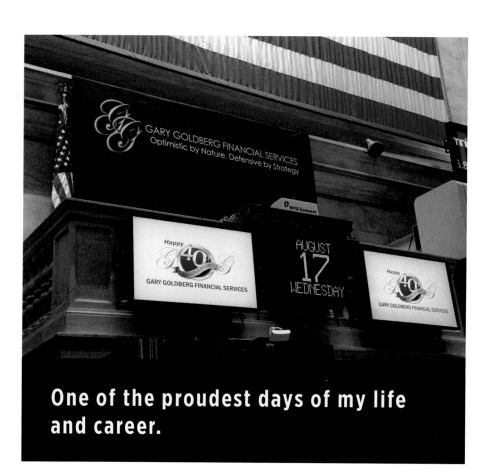

One of the proudest days of my life and career.

TAKING CARE OF THE CLIENT

Jack Mitchell, a clothier in Westport, Connecticut, says that you should hug your customer. Whether you take him literally is up to you, but his important message is to take care of your customer as if your business depends upon it – because it does.

He also says: People remember the experience, not the attributes

- Reimagine the customer experience.
- Starbucks is not about the coffee; it's about the experience.
- Provide the client experience that can't be matched.
- Develop a checklist to use for every element of the experience.
- Provide a total experience, not just a product sale, but a relationship beginning with the first moment.
- If a person considers becoming a client, it must be an effort by all people whose work affects the client to perform in an exemplary way.

- Clearly, our business at Gary Goldberg Financial Services isn't only about product features; it's about the client experience.
- Look for ways to give your client both simplicity and flexibility. The financial world can be both complicated as well as intimidating. We make it as clear & comfortable as possible.

- What's our strongest asset for growth? It's our client base, and referrals are the least expensive way of getting new clients. But they must be harvested. They don't just fall into your lap.

Charging for your services

When you establish a fee-based business as I did, you must convince your prospect that your services are worth it. In so doing, I came to realize that there is a distinction between people who are "frugal" and those who are "cheap."

Frugal people take pleasure in saving, while cheap people feel pained by spending. It is much easier to deal with a frugal client than a cheap one. I appreciate that everyone wants a good deal, but in the long run, a cheap client is very difficult to work with. Spendthrifts, on the other hand, will spend money without recognizing that spending money now means less spending later.

- Your client wants certain basics:
- A - Know me; B - Understand my needs; C - Make me feel important; D - Ask my opinion and E - Do something special for me. I would also add that they want you to stay in touch with them and don't delay any bad news if any develops. People want to be kept in the loop.
- Think about all the touch points where you can connect with your clients and work to make each one better at getting things done.

For instance, we've had various activities, such as a day at the Playland Amusement Park in Rye, New York. where as many as a thousand people would show up as my guests -- and that includes the children and grandchildren of our clients. We've also had special baseball evenings where our clients are invited by me to watch the local minor league team of the Tampa Bay Rays play. We attract about the same number of guests. We have a barbecue for our guests in the stands (down the right field line). I even throw out the first pitch every year. I usually get it over the plate, but I assure you the catcher doesn't have to soak his hand in ice after the catch! The benefit to us is that we meet their children and grandchildren. I'm proud to say that we now have four generations of clients.

- Look for opportunities to provide service, information, advice, support and product enhancements directly to the clients.

After getting a new client

What we do: Once you develop a new client relationship, you must keep that new client feeling special. The first 100 days is critical in making that great second impression. The client experience during that period can be the difference between them telling all their friends about you or feeling buyer's remorse. Don't first fold a new client into your book and go on to the next acquisition. In doing so, you are ignoring the referral opportunities that you can generate when you put a little extra effort into servicing that new client. You also make the client know that they are special, and allay any concerns that can develop in any new relationship.

Clients should feel that they are alumni of GGFS from their first day (i.e., a gift; a welcoming dinner; ideas for a lifetime connection, such as lectures and seminars; special dinners at my home, etc.). We give out a high quality letter opener (with our logo on it) to our clients and tell them, "You're going to get a lot of mail from us, and this will help open it up! It'll save you from breaking a nail." The cost is minimal, but sets you apart from other advisors that they might have had or still have.

A welcoming letter comes from me, and we make satisfaction calls a few weeks after signing on a new client. About a month later, we notify our clients about any upcoming client events and ask that new client to feel free to bring a friend with them who they feel could benefit from an introduction to our practice and our approach to money management.

By spending this extra effort in making sure that our new clients are receiving this extra level of service, we feel that we are opening the door to referral opportunities down the road by creating an advocate for our organization.

- We also use periodic get-togethers to strengthen our relationships.
- When the cash register goes "ca-ching," many companies lose sight of the other connections. (We don't, which is why I believe that we get so many referrals.)
- Create a comfortable, vibrant and uniquely local experience. Our mansion certainly contributes to that.
- Create warmth, openness, generosity, and a welcoming feeling. At our first meeting, I make sure to introduce as many members of the firm to our new client as possible.
- If you can, try to recognize a market that is often overlooked. In the financial industry I discovered that women were not approached or spoken to on an equal level as were their male counterparts. Ironically, they are more likely to become the inheritors in a family, and typically, they needed longer term planning. I remember years ago often hearing husbands say to their wives, "Don't worry your pretty little head about the finances, I'll take care of it." That's a big mistake! There's a reason Ozzie and Harriet is not on television anymore!
- Pass through the experience as if you were an outsider. It's

important, after a meeting with a client, to reflect on what you might have done better during that meeting. Criticize yourself and continue to improve.

- Benchmark the organization against those you don't compete with as well as those you do.
- Your welcoming face is your selling face. Smile before you greet your client. I actually do it to the back of the door of my office before I open it to greet my clients in the lobby! It sets the tone for my first words.

We consider the client experience so important that one of my assistants, Gina Neilson, who sits at the front desk and greets our clients, has a sign on her desk that says, "Director of First Impressions." And she takes her role very seriously.

- Think about your radio and Internet presence. I'm interviewed several times a week as a go-to source by a number of New York radio stations relating to the direction of the markets. If you are fortunate enough to be in a similar circumstance within your industry, let people know that's the case. It enforces your image as a knowledgeable professional who others seek insight and opinions from.
- People want to know that using our services will reduce their stress or anxiety level. We offer a respite from a client's financial tension and are therefore appreciated and even loved. Ultimately we are recommended to others.
- Be patient in explaining your products and services. People shy away from things they clearly don't understand. We take special care to make them feel better about their new relationship with us and explain the benefits of what they are about to purchase. Carefully explain what makes you different.

- "Cookie-cutter" or "one-size-fits-all" are terms of derision. Show what a customized experience is all about. At our firm, we emphasize that if you become our client that we will provide a "Just for you" service that no large company can offer. We offer unique programs and services without many confusing choices, and we guide the client towards their ultimate conclusion if they are indecisive. We have discovered that that is what people are looking for.

Most of the advertising budget should go towards existing clients. They become your sales people.

- Leverage your existing community of loyal clients. They already like you. They are easy to reach and ready to accept new offerings.
- Provide them with rewards that will increase their loyalty and encourage them to invite others into the circle.
- Investigate websites that may support or supplement your own Internet presence.
- Focus on the buying power of ethnic minorities and other diverse groups who could use your services. One of our advisors, Gerald Inman, is a former NFL player and has a big presence in the African-American community and within his church. He's a center of influence and revered by those who know him. He has given us entre' into his community, a diverse group that we otherwise might not have been able to offer our services to in the same way. Unfortunately, ethnic groups are often overlooked in our industry.
- Develop a database to track the interests and activities of your clients. Tailor your mailings and invitations to each crowd.
- Your most loyal clients are looking for new ways to connect with you.

CHAPTER 9

- When seeking new ways to serve clients, tap the creativity of all people connected with your occupation. You don't have to reinvent the wheel. You can figure out what has worked elsewhere, and apply it to your own business.
- There comes a time in the life of every organization when you must expand your products or services in order to increase revenues. You must have the desire to provide clients with benefits that they can't enjoy elsewhere. You won't find out what those are if you just stay in your office. Get out there and **"kick the bricks."**

Small things that will set you apart

Start or end an email or letter with the following phrases: "Great talking to you," "Give my best to," "You've been on my mind lately." It's important to start or finish letters with something personal.

- I'm calling to see how you are doing.
- I'm thinking about you...
- Is anything new going on?
- Does anything need attention?
- I always say, "Thank you for our relationship."
- Clients appreciate hand written thank-you notes.
- Put real stamps on personal notes.
- Know as much about your client as you do your product -- and act on it. Your products may change over time, but your relationship with your client can only be enhanced by showing them that you care.

Work to work, and the rest will follow. If it isn't about the money, it's fun to see how much comes your way. When your focus is on your client, the rest takes care of itself.

- You always want to under-promise and over-deliver.
- It typically costs between 5 to 8 times more to replace the sales revenue from a lost client than if you had not lost that client in the first place.
- If you provide an exceptional client experience, you can charge more. If a prospect or client does not appreciate the quality or service that they are paying for, it may be a bad fit. **The Four Seasons hotel is not competing with a Motel 6!**
- If you're thinking about going out on your own, ask your existing client base, on a scale of 0 – 10, 0 being the worst, how likely they would be to follow you or recommend you to others if you were to establish your own business. Also, ask them, "Since you're my number one priority, where would you like to see an improvement?"

The client experience must be at the top of the list in running your business. As I said, if you invest in your clients, the profits will follow.

- Pay particular attention to your largest accounts. There is the 80/20 rule – that 80% of your business will come from the top 20% of your clients. But be sure not to forget the other 80%.
- Drop a note to clients as to why this is a good time to add to their portfolio or to protect their portfolio if you think that it is. And don't forget to ask to see any other accounts that they might have elsewhere, that they might like for you to review.
- The best way to add to the top of the pyramid is from the bottom up. The best advertising is word-of-mouth.
- Your existing clients, when they are satisfied, become your best and least expensive source of new relationships.

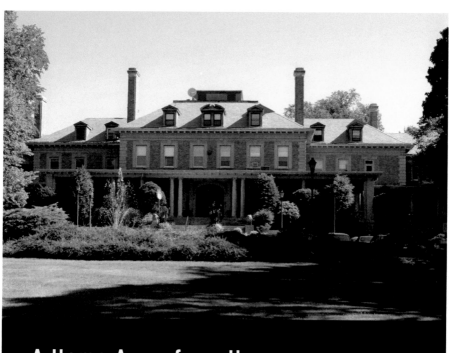

A Home Away from Home.
The Montebello Mansion
Final Office Location.

CHAPTER 10

MANAGING YOUR BUSINESS

*B*usyness, long hours and hard work do not necessarily equal success. A watch is no more than jewelry to an entrepreneur, and a way to make sure that they get to an appointment on time.

Make certain that you do the vital stuff. Build a great team of capable players who are excellent at the rest.

As far as keeping myself organized, my day starts very early. I do a four-mile outdoor jog every other day at around 6 a.m. and then I get to the office around 8 AM. I am also blessed with a fabulous staff. Two-third's of the firm's staff is service–oriented, and one-third is sales -- which is much different from the rest of my industry.

At this stage of our existence, and after 45 years, it's not difficult for our firm to get new clients, but it's very important to keep the current ones from going out the back door while bringing in new ones through the front. The majority of my service-oriented staff are trained registered reps, even if they're administrative assistants. I have encouraged that training, and no, I'm not afraid of them leaving me and becoming brokers somewhere else. I simply want them to pass their Series 7 exam in order to better service our clients by having more extensive knowledge.

My typical day is spent meeting with clients on an hourly basis. In our firm, we have an expression, "Lunch is for wimps." Yes, Gordon gecko said it in the movie "Wall Street" -- but we've adopted it! Furthermore, at the end of the day I will do an analysis of the cases I need to bring home with me. In the evening, I will often do several hours of work – and I do it because I love it. It is not work to me; work is something that you do that's not enjoyable. I have a very long day, but I don't look at it that way. I manage to spend a great deal of time with my wife, Joan, my children and grandchildren, and still frequently work on weekends, even at this stage of my career.

Delegate – You Can't Do It All

- Equate your inbox on your smart phone or iPad to the modern day mailroom and don't waste a lot of time in the mailroom when you should be out there being productive.
- When you delegate to someone else, it allows them to exercise their strengths and abilities and that's how you build an organization.
- My vital function in my firm is meeting with my clients, bringing in new clients from speaking engagements, including my radio show, and serving on the Executive and Investment Committee of my firm. Everything else is superfluous and potentially a distraction.

At Gary Goldberg Financial Services, Peter Dedel has been running our stock trading department for 38 years. Bill Krivicich has run our research department for 15 years. For 12 years we also had someone who was the face of the firm on TV so that I didn't have to spend my time going to TV studios. And Rich Kersting runs the sales and training department, and has been with me for 12 years.

I do the strategic planning and meet with clients all day long.

The four of us compose the Investment Committee as well as the Executive Committee, which focuses on the direction of the firm.

This approach has allowed me not to get caught up in doing things that are less productive throughout my day, so I can then focus on sales and the bottom line. That's also why my assistants, Bette Ellen Weiss and Oksana Kavka, are so important to me. In my firm, I am the rainmaker and should not be bogged down by tasks that others can and should do. More importantly, I trust the others. They all play a role in our success.

It's up to me to define where my efforts should go. That then becomes critical to the continued growth of my organization.

My conclusion, therefore, is to isolate a few essential functions and spend my time only on those. You must delegate everything else.

- How do you prioritize your vital functions? Warren Buffett had a strategy.
    - o A – Write down all your priorities
    - o B – Narrow it down to the top three
    - o C – Throw the rest of the list away
- If you have more than three priorities, you don't have any! It means saying "no" to interruptions.
- Saying "yes' to everything and everybody is easy. Saying "no" is difficult. It hurts people's feelings. But you must prioritize your own time and efforts to be a successful entrepreneur.

- In managing your time, when you say "yes" to something, you're actually saying "no" to something else. So you must prioritize.

A wonderful exercise is to play the "Yes and..." game with your colleagues. It encourages ideas and participation. It makes them listen carefully and expand on ideas already verbalized. Start by speaking about anything relating to the business. Keep the conversation going by saying to the next speaker in the group, "Yes, and..." Then have them introduce a new idea or comment that keeps the conversation going and makes everyone feel like they are contributing. It forces people to listen and stay engaged. We've done it at our weekly sales meetings.

Our clients get the benefit of these ideas

- Deal with people in an ethical fashion.
- Set goals for each day and each week and compare them against last week's goals.
- Everyone is important and they have to feel that way for the company to be successful.
- Outline goals for each person in your company. Write them down. Identify the areas that you want to improve upon and track the progress throughout the year.
- Make each and every "player on the team" feel important.
- Compliment a coworker for a job well done and smile at someone who is having a rough day.
- Business is about relationships.
- Don't succumb to analysis to paralysis.

Sometimes the best deals are the ones you don't make.
Don't voluntarily tie an anchor around your neck.

The difference between a good leader and a manager is the confidence it takes to react to the unanticipated event when it occurs with resolve and decisiveness.

I've learned as an entrepreneur while climbing the ladder of success that you have to ally yourself with someone with an understanding of your firm who you can respect the opinion of, and who is available; not a yes man, but someone who can act as an advisor in their area of expertise. They will help you in limiting your risk. Use their judgment along with your own. They can be your check and balance. You must trust them in relation to questions such as whether you're taking on too much risk, or moving too quickly. Allow them to advise, but not to make the ultimate decision. That rests with you, the entrepreneur. You as the founder must make the ultimate decision.

- Unless you have unlimited financial resources, avoid taking a chance that could be catastrophic if it fails. That way, you still have an opportunity to recover if you haven't made a ridiculous decision that didn't work. **Bad decisions** provide you with an opportunity to learn and not repeat.

Our clients get the benefit of these ideas

- The company culture starts at the top
- We're in the people business.
- No company flourishes without trust.
- Show your appreciation. Send flowers when you hire someone.

- Give a small bonus – after six months call that new person into your office and hand them a check.
- People are assets that pay dividends for their companies. My wife and I use our home for drinks and food after work for employees to gather in a relaxed atmosphere.
- Be a transparent company. Celebrate a great quarter. It creates a bond.
- Have an open-door policy. I keep my office door open when I'm not in a meeting.
- If there is a squabble, define it and address it early. Show a genuine desire to resolve the issue.
- Give away shirts with slogans and tote bags featuring your company. Your employees will wear them or use them with pride.
- Take an employee to dinner. Ask them questions. Find out what makes them tick. What are their aspirations? You'd be amazed how you can find a diamond in the rough when you get to know someone and their capabilities.
- Get rid of the "us" versus "them" culture within your organization.
- Be involved in community events. It should be at the core of your business. Take part in charitable events. Give back. It makes employees feel good about who they work for.
- I use the mansion to host events. Sunday brunch on the Terrace; A fashion show for breast cancer; and fundraisers for not-for-profit organizations (i.e., the Tommy John Foundation as well as the Ramapo Teachers' Organization have been recent events.)
- Even if people don't become our clients, they will know about us from this type of positive exposure.
- People should work as long as they have the passion and can contribute to the company.

- Encourage people to have fun at work.
- I look forward to going to work after all these years.
- Retain and market the equity of a long-standing and local brand-name. We've been doing it for almost 50 years. That's a statement right there. We use it!

There are two types of ownership in a business
   A) legal ownership and
   B) a sense of ownership – one where a manager should feel like an owner, but you, the owner, get the final word.

- Success is the power of all of us.
- Money is not the main reason people choose where they work for life.
- Give them the opportunity to earn more and learn more.
- Give them tickets to something that they are passionate about.
- Marketing should gather data along with census information about your employees (i.e., their birthdays, hobbies and family member's names), and use it.
- Integrity must encompass how you operate. That is especially true when it comes to finances.
- Clients are thirsting for relationship driven companies.
- Try to reach the top executives of a company. If the top executives of the company become your clients, others will follow. So service the top.
- When you grow, you must not forget the principles the company was founded on.
- Bad times hit all businesses, and when they do, you can't cutback things that a client will notice. Remember, if a key person was to leave the company, clients will notice. It would be like going to Disneyland and not seeing Mickey Mouse.

- Pay your people well. Everyone has bills to pay.
- It's not location, location, location. It's service, service and service.
- A sudden development is not a problem. It's an opportunity or a challenge.
- In a troubled relationship, almost always, you tend to hang on too long, hoping the situation will improve. Usually it doesn't. With your employees, let them go, or let them grow.
- Create an environment where everyone feels comfortable with contributing ideas.

It's not who is right, but what is right that is of importance.

- Being classy is about moving the spotlight away from yourself. As I mentioned, when I was invited to go on a TV business network, I found someone within our firm who was both knowledgeable and was TV friendly and could do it for me. That way I didn't have to spend half of my work day going to a studio to appear on the air for three minutes. It also made him feel important.
- Nothing gives one person so much advantage over another as to remain cool and calm under all circumstances.
- Pressure is something you feel when you don't know what you're doing or how to get there.
- Don't forget to appreciate the people who help you along the way.
- There are no calluses on our backs from patting each other. Let people know how important they are. Keep patting them on the back. It goes a long way.

Everybody that works in the company has to be involved in selling your services. Ask them "What have you done to bring a client into our firm? What have you done to sell our firm to others? What have you done to make that client of ours happy."

You have a role. If you don't know what that role is, you need to find out!

The Legs We Stand On

When I built my company, my attitude was:

- A business venture is only as good as the legs it stands on. The legs this venture stands on are the people who work with us.
- We will accept our employees as long as we are all going in the same direction. Some may travel at a hundred miles per hour, some at 65, but everybody must move in the same direction.
- If you're going to run a department for me, I will give you great latitude. But I want you to tell me about things. I have regular meetings with my upper level staff where they will tell me what they'd like, but the ultimate decision is mine. (It's my checkbook.)
- Don't outgrow the ability of people to take you to the next level. It's their responsibility to do so. It's why you pay them well.

Jack Welch was voted Fortune's CEO of the 20th Century. Why? Because when he saw something that wasn't working right, he reacted quickly and did something about it. And the entire organization followed suit.

The secret of our success in this venture is that we have realized that we may not be that smart, and because we may not be that smart, we have learned that we must listen. By listening, we learned that the client dictates who we must be, what we must be, what our product must be and what services we must give to them. We have now successfully listened and responded for more than 45 years.

CHAPTER 10

To Gary Goldberg
With best wishes,

George Bush

41ˢᵗ U.S. President, George H. W. Bush.

CHAPTER 11

BEING A LEADER

M any entrepreneurs start off by themselves, or might have a partner or two. But at a certain point, there's a transition. When you start hiring employees, you are now in a position to influence others. Your vision has to become their vision in order for your business to succeed.

Some people can't make that transition, but others thrive on it. If you're good at it, there's not much in the business world that's more satisfying.

- Being a leader means making everyone around you better.
- Being a leader is 24/7. You never turn it off.
- A secret to success is how you treat people.
- To be a leader, you must empower others.
- The first step to success is to position your idea so that your success is everyone's success.
- Open, honest communication is the foundation of dealing with people.
- A good leader will make his team comfortable with a change before he puts it in place.
- Remember in every relationship, you can affect the other

person's life. Don't treat the discussions lightly.
- Don't focus on short term victories or defeats. Focus on the long term picture.
- Lead – and negotiate -- by understanding people's wants and needs.
- I learned that I never stop learning.

If you get 80% of the facts, that is usually enough to make a decision. To get the last 20% could take forever. Make a decision and get on with it. Don't be afraid to make mistakes. The only time people don't make mistakes is when they're asleep. If you're wrong, admit it and try another approach.

- The first time to become a team player is your first day on the job. We make sure to introduce the individual to all of the other members of the firm.
- As a leader, asking "dumb" questions is always better than making big mistakes.
- Never assume you're doing anything in isolation. Always assume there will be a reaction from those who will be effected.
- As a leader, you must explain why change is necessary.
- If your people make mistakes, let them tell you how they're going to correct things.
- Think about it and then adjust.
- Honesty from the top down allows people to perform at their best.

The best motivation is appreciation.

For instance, we had a new person in marketing, and I went to her office and told her what a great job she was doing. I also told other members of my firm to stop by and thank her.

- The entire organization must understand and embrace the vision to be successful.
- Positive reinforcement from a leader is most critical when times are tough.
- When you see a person show up for work, and go through the motions and just collect their paycheck, they are never going to help the company.
- If someone leaves a job, treat them as if you might work with them again.

A true leader should guide and help, not demand and demean.

- Respect and appreciation are what really drives employees.
- Show your employees love; don't instill fear. Let them know they are really wanted. Tell them you believe in them.
- When you are most concerned, that is when you need to exude the most confidence.
- Worry about the next play, not a past play.
- In a business negotiation, let the best idea win, whether it's yours or not.
- Be the boss you wish you had.
- Invite your employees to be part of a focus group for the betterment of the company.
- Communicate to all employees what business we are in and what our philosophy is as a company (i.e., providing quality "money management for real people," something that our industry is lacking).
- Ask what we could be doing better for the client. They may see things that upper management will never understand.
- There is importance in helping the community. Make

charitable contributions. (I set up a charitable foundation. I received tax benefits in establishing it and gratification from donating the proceeds.)

I have found that actions (rather than just words) show an employee that they are valuable. It motivates them to do even better in the future. And giving individual recognition can be more important than bonuses. The great reward comes in recurring acknowledgment that the person contributed to making something meaningful happen. Also, don't underestimate the power of praise, particularly in front of others. If it's not made public, the recognition loses much of its impact and defeats its purpose.

Some inexpensive ways that I have said a special thank you to employees and bolstered their morale:

1. - Dinner with their spouse at my home
2. - A massage, facial or manicure
3. - A gift certificate
4. - A champagne brunch with their spouse
5. - Tickets to an event with a limo ride included

I have also found when rewarded with time off – a free day, a two-hour lunch or a three-day weekend – it brings the employee back refreshed and smiling. Sometimes, I will even write a check on the spot to a person, not for sales, but for just doing a good job!

- I always have tried to encourage the people around me to aim for a leadership role. That has worked in building the depth of our organization and has kept people here for many years.

You must learn how to delegate authority. It is a very difficult thing to do. You have to stop shoveling the snow; you have to motivate others to do the shoveling. You can't do everything yourself. Identify what you are good at, then give the others the tools to succeed and trust that they will succeed. Put together a team that you can trust, who will eventually follow in your footsteps.

- Getting caught up in the minutiae will preclude you from thinking about how to make the business better.
- I want the best idea to work, even if it's not mine.
- In dealing with my employees, rarely do I raise my voice. If I am going to yell, I want to make sure my voice is heard. If you yell too often, you won't get anyone's attention when you raise your voice.
- When I was building my business, and even now, there was no job too insignificant for me to do if it needed to get done.
- I have concluded that you need three things to be a real success:
  - o **Talent**
  - o **Intelligence**
  - o **A work ethic**

- A leader must stop, pin their ears back and hear what people have to say. Practice listening, not just sometimes, but all of the time. Provide an atmosphere of give and take.
- Be a leader who is calm, confident and clear about where you want to go and where you want to take others.
- You have to manage yourself in order to lead others. The fact is, the majority of our communication is non-verbal. People will react to what they see as much as what they hear.
- If you see yourself as a leader, think "What are others seeing in me and in what direction am I leading?"

Tough Decisions

My upbringing and success as an entrepreneur was a process of coming from a place – my family, my neighborhood – and then creating something that was new. There's a kind of self-confidence that comes with each and every step along the way. That helped prepare me to be a leader and make tough decisions.

There comes a time when one must take a position that is neither safe, nor polite, nor popular. But you must take it because it is right. As a leader, you must have the courage to accept responsibility. If you are looking for excuses or someone to blame, you will never get to where you are trying to go.

- You have to learn to deal with the consequences. You have to prepare for anything – praise, criticism -- for the sake of yourself and for the people who count on you.
- Leadership is about pulling, pushing and moving, not for sitting.
- The core of leadership – first you say it and then you do it.
- A leader can offer counsel and make demands. He can criticize a colleague for a dumb mistake and then throw an arm over their shoulder moments later, or have a drink after work or breakfast in the morning.

Self-evaluation is very important

You may not be as good as you think you are. Studies consistently show that we often think we're better at things than we are. In fact, in business, three fourths of leaders probably think they're in the top 10% of their field. Guess what? That math doesn't work.

I recall when I was a freshman at Bard College and submitted my first book report to my freshman English Professor (Dr. Cohen). I was so proud of what I turned in that I couldn't wait for the following week to see my grade. I knew that I nailed it.

When the following week arrived, I turned to the back page of my submission expecting to see an A+. Instead, one of the more meaningful comments that I have ever learned from was summed up in one word, "Ughh!!" I quickly learned that I was not as good as I thought I was, a lesson that I took into the future as a business founder and CEO.

Therefore, stop believing you're very good and get very good.

Miami Beach Police Chief and family honoring mom for saving a life.
(From left to right: My son Andrew Goldberg, Gary Goldberg, Police Chief, Rose Goldberg and my son Mark Goldberg)

CHAPTER 12

ODD JOBS, LIFE LESSIONS

As I said earlier in this book, I went to law school, but only for a year and a half before dropping out. I didn't like it, and decided I wanted to do something else, but I wasn't sure what it was going to be. So in the interim, if you can believe it, I got a job sorting and grading lizard and alligator skins. I'd separate them for the belt manufacturers, the hand bag manufacturers, and the shoe manufacturers. It wasn't the kind of job where you needed a college education, or a year and a half of law school. But you do what you have to do to get a job.

After my boss turned down my request for a $5 a week raise, I quit. So after the lizard skin job, my uncle Lou, who had some real estate in some rough, lower income neighborhoods in the Bronx, gave me a job as a rent collector. Back then, rent collection wasn't computerized; you'd knock on doors, go to the Kelly home, or the Johnson home, or the Schwartz home, and they would give you cash in an envelope. I'd knock on the door and often be invited in. An Irish family would offer me Irish soda bread, an Italian family focaccia bread, whatever they had. I'd sit at their kitchen table, schmooze for a few minutes, and then collect the rent, $60 or $70. But it became particularly dangerous in certain neighborhoods. I would have to walk around with the superintendent of the building, and usually a German Shepherd dog in tow, who would accompany us for our protection. He would growl and be there for defensive purposes in these bad neighborhoods. It's hard to believe that I now own the Montebello Mansion. Only in America.

I mention this because in the financial industry, there are two categories of backgrounds, "spooners" and "streeters." You can identify people by the kind of bonds their neighborhood knew. There are three kinds of bonds: there are treasury bonds, for the people that came out of the rich neighborhoods in Connecticut or Park Avenue; there were E bonds for average people like my family – you bought a bond for $18.75, they matured at $25 in ten years and you'd give them out for Bar Mitzvahs, Christenings and graduations. Then there was the third category: bail bonds, which were popular in some of the neighborhoods I worked in!

It's a lesson for any entrepreneur. It doesn't matter where you come from, but understand how hard your clients have worked to obtain what they have been able to save. Not being a silver- spooner, I am able to relate to the average person, and they can relate to me.

You can rise from the ashes.

I learned another lesson when I was a waiter at age 21 at a hotel called the Laurel in the Pines in Lakewood, New Jersey. The dance instructor at this hotel, who was my age, was dating the daughter of the owner of the hotel, while I was dating the other daughter. In fact, they were twins. The twins' parents loved me because I was going to be the successful lawyer that they always envisioned for their daughter. The dancer on the other hand, whose name was Neil, was nothing more than a dance instructor to them, with no apparent future ahead of himself, and they didn't want their daughter wasting their time with him.

So I was dating Nancy, and he was dating Beth. In fact, when not working at the hotel, we would double date. But I had to pick up both girls, as if I was taking them both out because the girls' parents would not welcome him. I'd ride down the elevator in this beautiful high-rise hotel that they permanently resided in which was located in a beautiful part of Brooklyn. If you can imagine, I had to sneak his date out because their parents didn't want her to have anything to do with him. He got the last laugh though, eventually. He changed his name from Neil Bogatz to Neil Bogart and became one of the biggest music producers during the rise of bubblegum pop music. In fact, he became a titan in the industry. The lesson is, don't underestimate anyone and where their talent can take them.

During that period, I was working the New Year's weekend at the hotel, and as I said, I was dating Nancy. The maître d' of the dining room told me on New Year's Eve day. "Gary, I need you to work the midnight shift." I said, "Izzy, I'm not working the midnight shift. I'm dating Nancy and I'm going to be with her for New Year's. Give me a Break!"

He said, "No, I need you." The owner of the hotel, the girl's father, walked by, and I said, "Izzy wants me to work the midnight shift, but I want to be with Nancy. Please tell him it's okay." He said, 'No, it's not okay. If Izzy wants you to work, you have to work.'" I said, "No, I want to be with Nancy and if you make me work I'm going to quit." He said, "You have to work. Or quit." So I quit, stupidly and impulsively and immaturely.

Why do I tell you this story? Well, as it turned out, if you quit on New Year's Eve, the next day is checkout day, when everybody leaves and all the waiters get their tips. So I ended up making nothing for the week. Furthermore, as it turned out I was not allowed to date Nancy for New Year's Eve because her father prevented it. Ultimately, I got on the bus in Lakewood, New Jersey, on New Year's Eve and went down to Times Square, spending New Year's Eve alone with my dear friend Arthur and the Times Square crowd. No Nancy, and no money to show for a week's worth of work. The lesson:

Be careful what you do in making rash decisions.
They can come back and bite you.

CHAPTER 12

My sons Mark and Justin Goldberg, with my wife Joan.

CHAPTER 13

THE ENTREPRENEUR SPIRIT

G reat expressions that I have learned in my life:

- You can only have two things in life, reasons or results. (Reasons don't count.)
- Before you can break out of prison, you must first realize that you're locked up in one.
- If you don't like the direction the river is flowing, don't jump in.
- The cowards never start and the weak die along the way.
- Some want the fire, but they don't want to chop the wood.
- There are many things I want, but few things that I need.
- If you have a college degree (and you're a money manager), you can be absolutely sure of only one thing; that you have a college degree.
- Most of the time we don't communicate, we just take turns talking.
- Look for opportunities, not guarantees.
- You need to feel the fire in your belly.
- You don't make an omelette without breaking the egg

My favorite philosophy: **If it is to be, it is up to me!**

- Accountants see risk – entrepreneurs see opportunity.
- Entrepreneurs who have cash balances sitting around doing nothing make me pause.
- The road is littered with cautious, conservative and prudent entrepreneurs who never get started. Keep your foot on the gas pedal. And be sure to look through the windshield. Don't focus on the rear view mirror.
- Business is war without bullets.
- Everyone makes mistakes, it's how you handle them that matters!
- Own up to your mistakes and make a few adjustments, and move on. Anything short of that is counter-productive and self-serving.
- The saying, "I'm bitter right now" is meaningless. Work hard to change one letter -- the "i" to and "e," and you will see amazing results.

I took some risks that looked outrageous:

- I took the chances
- I borrowed heavily at times.
- I mortgaged my house.
- I mortgaged my office building.
- I borrowed against my life insurance.
- I used my car as collateral.
- I made deals that looked bad on paper.
- I borrowed even more.

But I had confidence in myself. In the end, taking the risks, and reaching for perfection, not necessarily achieving it, was worth the effort.

- If no one ever took risks, Michelangelo might have painted the Sistine floor.
- Don't even think about stopping until you get there.
- A tiger hunts best when he's hungry.

Believe in your product: Get ready for the struggles and competitions that lie ahead. If you believe in your product, it becomes irresistible to others.

Innovate – and keep innovating

A pitfall that an entrepreneur falls into is that they may stick to the status quo. That may work in the short term, but the world around us is always changing and unless you adjust, you can become a victim of outside forces. I found an educational void in my industry when it came to knowledge of financial matters even though people were accumulating more wealth in the 1970s. I started teaching adult classes at the community college in the evenings and started doing dinner seminars before they became common place.

- When I started GGFS, I didn't sit around theorizing. I first started building a business and making my presence felt.
- There's no growth without discontent. You can turn discontent into something positive. It's much better than sitting back on your laurels.
- Therapists are expensive friends. Instead, talk to your family and colleagues to get their input – and respect it. You might

find some great wisdom if you listen to them. I've been blessed with a wife, Joan, that I can bounce ideas off of and get from her valuable insight. I couldn't do it without her.

- Your success – or lack of it -- is often measured by your inability to complete things. Follow up, and follow through. Understand, other people are counting on that.
- It's not enough to make a good product or provide a great service. You need to explain it to your client that it is a way to improve their life.
- If you can, tell a story. In my presentations, I try to personalize my speeches with stories.
- When I grew up, there were no organized activities for kids. We took care of ourselves. What a valuable lesson there was in that!
- We didn't score ourselves on the value or number of possessions that we owned. Unfortunately, much of our current culture does.
- Entrepreneurs should focus on transforming an existing industry or part of one and create a much better product or service as seen through the customer's eyes.
- There must be the concept of "there must be a better way."
- You must deliver a lights out customer experience and you will if you concentrate on it.
- Marketing innovation doesn't have to be in the product itself; it can be in the "packaging" or the service.
- Promote "The exceptional client experience." BMW did it – "The Ultimate Driving Machine."
- Thomas Edison is credited with a great expression: "Genius is 1% inspiration, 99% perspiration. And he provided us all with a lights out experience. (Pardon the pun.)
- Best way to have a good idea is to have lots of ideas.
- An entrepreneur must work and train like an Olympic athlete.

CHAPTER 13

Difference is, you don't have to be young. Hard work is an essential element in being successful.

- Entrepreneurs need to be optimists.
- The age of entrepreneurs has gone up to the Baby Boomer level. Boomers have a vast reservoir of experience and talent from prior jobs and they have more money than the "HENRY" group – High Earners, Not Rich Yet. They should be your major source of clients, at least in the financial and investment business.
- Peter Drucker, the management expert, said, "People who don't take risks generally make about two mistakes a year; people who do take risks generally make about two mistakes a year."
- At some point, entrepreneurs are very likely to find themselves in a situation where they will need to sharply fine tune or completely redefine themselves in order to survive.
- **If you really aren't a risk taker, then you need to think twice about whether you're the right person to become an entrepreneur.**
- At some point, entrepreneurs are not motivated by money or fame, but the love of what they do.
- **In a startup company, you're going to make mistakes; it's how you handle the mistakes and learn from them that will enable you to survive a mistake.**
- Mistakes are not the end of the world. As I said, they provide you with an opportunity to learn.

Entrepreneurship and the desire to be one has a downside. It sets expectations and shapes behaviors in ways that convince people to chase after things they may not need or want, while overlooking the costs of this pursuit. It's why I have called this book, "**How Badly Do You Want It?**"

Think long and hard before jumping into the world of entrepreneurship. Many people have all of the trappings of a wildly successful professional and personal life, but stew in anxiety and unhappiness and feel that they have to gamble and go out on their own. The downside, of course, is that one may take on a lot of debt, and failure can undermine their physical and mental health while disrupting their financial and family life. I strongly suggest that before you take that step and start out on your own venture, you take inventory of the impact it is going to have on you, your spouse, your children and your finances. Look before you leap, and discuss it with your family. Let them know the ride they may be in for. It's only fair to them.

- You can't do passion half-way. Living your passion means you're all in.
- A successful person is usually an average person who took a chance.
- I put everything on the line to create my company.
- Ask yourself, "Do you sincerely want to be rich?"
- I am able to point to GGFS and say "I made that." It has made my life meaningful.
- Weak men wait for opportunities; strong men make them.
- Entrepreneurship consists of challenges and crises.

The "Entrepreneur" – says give me the ball. They are not afraid to take the last shot when the game is on the line and the buzzer is about to go off. They have the passion and the confidence to win.

- Is this how you really want to spend your time? Ask yourself and be truthful with yourself.
- It is a calling – not just a career.
- In a calling like entrepreneurship, the disappointments act as fuel, and the highs are like nothing you have ever felt.

CHAPTER 13

- Entrepreneurs are always fighting an uphill battle. But success is an overwhelming gratification.

   Entrepreneurs dip into their pockets to make sure everyone has a job.

- What the world really needs are dreamers who do it. That's the entrepreneur. Don't fail by not trying.

For 9 years I would pay someone to come to my house twice a week, and teach me Kung Fu. They would beat the heck out of me, and I would pay for that pain. Can you believe it! But, it taught me:

- **Discipline**
- **Endurance**
- **Concentration**
- **Perseverance**

   Everything an entrepreneur needs to succeed.

My beautiful wife Joan.

CHAPTER 14

AN ENTREPRENEUR'S PAYDAY

A s I started getting older, and I had no partners or children in my company, I decided to consider selling GGFS. One reason was that I wanted to make sure I could be around after the sale, and to make sure there was no diminution of the values that I had worked so hard to make as part of the firm that I created. Another reason was that when a company becomes a disproportionate amount of your net worth, as mine was, it became a good idea to monetize something that is usually illiquid.

So I reached out to an investment banking firm and asked them to find me a buyer. I wanted to value my company at a certain number, but I also wanted to maintain the company values. So I gave them the criteria: 1) Take your time in finding the right buyer; 2) I come with the deal; and 3) nobody gets fired.

They brought me seven potential acquirers. Three were public companies – I dismissed them outright because I felt that they would fire people. And I had discussions with the remaining four to see who would be a good fit. I allowed the investment bankers to advise me, but ultimately, it's up to the entrepreneur to make the final decision.

Ultimately, the company that made me the most attractive offer convinced me to sell to them because they said, "We'll let you run the company. If you see us twice a year, it'll be a lot because we're not in the money management business. We'll let you do your thing." They went along with anything I wanted. They wrote me the biggest check I'd ever received.

Now the reality is that when you get a check like that, the money goes to various places. It all doesn't go into your bank account. A certain amount goes to the government, and that was the biggest check I ever had to write. I also had some mortgages on real estate that I decided to pay off. And in building the business over the years I incurred certain other debts that I was able to pay off. I also decided to take my payout over a number of years so I could spread out the taxes. As part of the transaction, I took back an interest bearing note at a very fair interest rate.

But to be able to cash that check and see the return on my original $5,000 investment, well, it was a good day to see the fruits of my labor come to fruition.

Working with another company

There are times when working with another company makes sense. You can acquire a capability that is very much-needed. The ongoing business of both companies must be profitable. There should be a synergy in the venture. The company may be more specialized than you are, or a company you can learn from, or one you can leverage from. But the companies must be compatible in values: the philosophy should ultimately be similar to what you believe in.

Final Thoughts

- It's ok to take on the difficult, but don't take on the impossible.
- While you focus on the bottom line, don't ignore the human element of business. You effect people's lives, either your colleagues, your clients or your family with your decisions.
- Having to fire somebody is often an acknowledgment that you made a mistake. However, you owe it to the company & it's survival to hold people accountable to the highest possible standards. Admit your mistakes when you make them. Simply put, I have never bought a pencil without an eraser on it.
- When you make money, that's fine. When you spend it wisely or give it to charity, that's fine, you can always make it back in some endeavor. But what you can't make more of is time.
- Some people take ridiculous chances with their money & make poor decisions by not doing the proper analysis. You must analyze the landscape and know your surroundings. Know what you're getting yourself into, and have a plan to extricate yourself if you need to.
- A lot of people are afraid of falling down and hurting themselves along the way. You've got to be able to take the lumps.
- Entrepreneurship is brutal. It's survival of the fittest. It gets down to a basic question & simple answer – What's a successful business? More money coming in than going out. If it's the other way around eventually you're out of business. It's as simple as that. Also, if you have a good idea but if you execute it poorly, you will also go broke. The talented entrepreneur has the idea, puts the team together, utilizes his/her capital properly & executes in gradual stages.

- Think about what the experience for your client should be and how you can improve the experience and in fact make it as ideal as possible.
- I have had a positive impact on thousands of people. It has made my career and my legacy so very worthwhile.
- Don't underpay your people. There's a saying "Minimum pay, minimum talent." Also, you must provide upside mobility & opportunities.
- While I have worked harder than anyone I know in my organization over the years, **I can't say, and will never say that I am self-made**. To make that claim would be an insult to all of the people who have helped me get to where I am. I'm just one man. I will take credit for assembling the right individuals, while at the same time, I am a collage of many people's efforts.
- Your success is built on relationships. Relationships are built on character. If you have talent and integrity, clients will come to you. I always feel that when I develop a relationship with a client, I have a moral contract with that client and with my profession to do what is right.
- A successful business evolves from satisfied clients and their referrals. Grow your company by doing the right thing. I've learned early on how important it is to love the work that I was doing. Yes, sometimes I will look back and ask myself how did I become so fortunate in finding such a rewarding path to follow for my life's work? How did this happen?
- I'm still expected to get up in the morning, get to my office and get to work. And at the end of the day, I have a smile on my face. How many people can say that?

CHAPTER 14

Conclusion

I've offered you some stories about critical moments in my life and shared how I managed through the many years since I founded my company in 1972. I have learned many lessons and continue to learn more along the way.

Every one of us has a unique journey. I hope that this book helps you find and follow your own. I have chosen, in managing my firm, to utilize an approach that allows dialogue and idea development from my colleagues. It is the opposite of what I would call "command and control leadership," which does not allow others to think, create or generate new ideas, which hinders the growth of an organization.

I want each person in my firm to think like an entrepreneur. I have created an atmosphere where others can create and insert their own meaning and even invent their own innovative ideas and actions rather than follow the ones that I alone may be envisioning.

I created GGFS from virtually nothing. I breathed life into it, nurtured it through tough times, brought it back from the dead several times and then watched it stand on its own two feet. When I look at the Montebello Mansion I'm able to say, "I built this." (Of course, not literally -- I wasn't around in 1901!)

I have given opportunities to my employees and their families to help them achieve their most important personal and professional goals, and helped my clients provide a legacy to their children and grandchildren.

My biggest regret is that I can't do it all over again and relive the whole thing.

*　　*　　*　　*　　*　　*

Remember this: You can never exceed the dream without having it in the first place. But you need to ask yourself,
"How badly do you want it?"

*　　*　　*　　*　　*　　*

CHAPTER 14

ABOUT THE AUTHOR

Gary M. Goldberg is the founder and Chief Executive Officer of Gary Goldberg Financial Services which he started in 1972. Since then, Mr. Goldberg has helped thousands of investors achieve their retirement goals. In addition to serving as the firm's CEO, Mr. Goldberg also hosts one of America's longest continually running financial radio talk show, Money Matters. As host of **Money Matters**, Mr. Goldberg is able to personally interview some of today's most influential political and business leaders, giving him a unique advantage to gain first-hand insight into their thoughts and feelings about current market and socio-economic conditions.

Made in the USA
Middletown, DE
21 December 2018